ISBN 978-1-5279-8555-1
PIBN 10150390

𝕾tate of 𝕴owa
1920

PRIMARY AND GENERAL

ELECTION LAWS

PREPARED UNDER THE DIRECTION OF

W. C. RAMSAY

SECRETARY OF STATE

EX LIBRIS

ELE

State of Iowa
1920

PRIMARY AND GENERAL

ELECTION LAWS

PREPARED UNDER THE DIRECTION OF

W. C. RAMSAY

SECRETARY OF STATE

Published by
THE STATE OF IOWA
Des Moines

NOMINATIONS AND PRIMARY ELECTIONS.

Date of Primary Election:

General, on first Monday in June.

Municipal, on last Monday in February in years when municipal election is held.

In cities under commission form of government, on second Monday preceding general municipal election.

Nomination papers, date for filing:

County officers, at least 30 days before primary election.

State officers, at least 40 days before primary election.

Representative in congress, at least 40 days before primary election.

Members of general assembly, at least 40 days before primary election.

United States senator, at least 40 days before primary election.

Presidential elector, at least 40 days before primary election.

Nomination papers, place for filing:

County officers, with county auditor.

State officers, with secretary of state.

Representative in congress, with secretary of state.

Members of general assembly, with secretary of state.

United States senator, with secretary of state.

Presidential elector, with secretary of state.

List of persons who have completed nomination papers certified by secretary of state to each county auditor at least 30 days before primary election.

Proclamation by county auditor, following above certification, giving time of holding the primary election, hours when polls will be open, and offices for which candidates are to be nominated.

Polls open:

In cities where registration is required, from 7:00 a. m. to 8:00 p. m.

In all other precincts, from 9:00 a. m. to 8:00 p. m.

M144077

Nomination on more than one ticket:
    Candidate must forthwith file with proper officer a written declaration indicating party designation for official ballot.

Filing of objections to nomination papers or certificates:
    With secretary of state, not less than 20 days before election.
    With other officers, not less than 8 days before election.

Withdrawal of nomination by filing written request:
    With secretary of state 30 days before election (16 days if a special election).
    With county auditor 15 days before election (12 days if a special election).
    With clerk 12 days before election (12 days if a special election).

Filing of certificates of nomination and nomination papers (nomination by convention or petition):
    For state, congressional, judicial and legislative offices, with secretary of state not more than 60 nor less than 40 days before election.
    For offices in cities and towns, with clerks not more than 40 nor less than 15 days before election.
    For all other offices, with the county auditor not more than 60 nor less than 30 days before election.

Canvass by board of supervisors, as county canvassing board:
    Second Tuesday next following the primary election.

Canvass by executive council, as state canvassing board:
    Second Monday after primary election.

List of nominees certified by secretary of state to each county auditor not less than 15 days before general election.

Statement of candidacy and petition for office of mayor or councilman in cities under commission form of government to be filed with city clerk at least 10 days before primary election.

Petition for nomination for office of councilman in cities under city manager plan to be filed with city or town clerk 10 days before election.

REGISTRATION.

In cities of 6,000 or more (including cities under special charter), registers hold continuous session for 2 days (in presidential years 3 days) from 8:00 a. m. to 9:00 p. m. in the usual voting places, beginning on second Thursday prior to any general, city or special election.

On election day registers meet, at place convenient to voting place, while polls are open, for those unable to register previously.

CONVENTIONS.

Judicial conventions:

State, not less than one nor more than two weeks after the regular state party convention.

District, not earlier than the first Thursday nor later than the fifth Thursday following the county convention.

County convention:

Fourth Saturday following the primary election.

District convention:

Not earlier than the first nor later than the fifth Thursday following the county convention.

State convention:

Not earlier than the first nor later than the fifth Wednesday following the county convention. .

GENERAL ELECTION.

Date:

General, on Tuesday, next after the first Monday in November.

Municipal, on last Monday in March.

Proclamation of governor, designating offices to be filled:

At least 30 days before general or special election.

Polls open:

In cities where registration is required, from 7:00 a. m. to 7:00 p. m.; in other voting places, from 8:00 a. m. to 7:00 p. m.

Canvass by board of supervisors, as county canvassing board:

On Monday after the general election.

Canvass by executive council, as state canvassing board:

On the twentieth day after the general election.

STATEMENT OF EXPENSES.

Candidates at any primary, municipal or general election must file statement of expenses within 10 days after such election:

For municipal or county office, with the county auditor. (For elective offices in cities under commission form of government and cities under city manager plan, see §§ 1056-a32 and 1056-b11.)

For other offices, with the secretary of state.

Chairmen of each party central committee must file statement of receipts and expenditures within 10 days after election:

For state and district central committees, with the secretary of state.

For county central committees, with the county auditor.

TABLE OF CONTENTS

DIVISION VI—VACANCIES IN OFFICE.

DIVISION VII—NOMINATIONS BY PRIMARY ELECTION.

PRIMARY AND GENERAL ELECTION LAWS

DIVISION XII—CANVASS OF VOTES.

DIVISION XIII—VOTING MACHINES.

CONSTITUTIONAL PROVISIONS

ARTICLE 2—RIGHT OF SUFFRAGE.

Section 1. **Electors.** Every male citizen of the United States, of the age of twenty-one years, who shall have been a resident of this state six months next preceding the election, and of the county in which he claims his vote, sixty days, shall be entitled to vote at all elections which are now or hereafter may be authorized by law.

Sec. 2. **Privileged from Arrest.** Electors shall, in all cases except treason, felony, or breach of the peace, be privileged from arrest on the days of election, during their attendance at such elections, going to and returning therefrom.

Sec. 3. **From Military Duty.** No elector shall be obliged to perform military duty on the day of election, except in time of war or public danger.

Sec. 4. **Persons in Military Service.** No person in the military, naval, or marine service of the United States shall be considered a resident of this state by being stationed in any garrison, barrack, or military or naval place or station within this state.

Sec. 5. **Disqualified Persons.** No idiot or insane person, or person convicted of any infamous crime, shall be entitled to the privilege of an elector.

Sec. 6. **Ballot.** All elections by the people shall be by ballot.

Sec. 7. **General Election.** The general election for state, district, county and township officers in the year 1916 shall be held in the same month and on the same day as that fixed by the laws of the United States for the election of presidential electors, or of president and vice-president of the United States; and thereafter such election shall be held at such time as the general assembly may by law provide.

ELECTIONS AND OFFICERS

DIVISION I.

TIME OF ELECTION AND TERM OF OFFICE.

Section 1057-a. General election. The general election for state, district, county and township officers shall be held throughout the state on Tuesday, next after the first Monday in November in the year nineteen hundred six and each two years thereafter. [31 G. A., ch. 36, § 2.]

Sec. 1058. Special election. Special elections authorized by any law, or held to supply vacancies in any office to be filled by the vote of the qualified voters of the entire state, or of any district, county or township, may be held at the time designated by such law, or by the officer authorized to order such election. [C. '73, § 574; R., § 460.]

Sec. 1061. Proclamation. At least thirty days before any general election, the governor shall issue his proclamation, designating all the offices to be filled by the vote of all the electors of the state, or by those of any congressional, legislative or judicial district, and, in the years required by article ten, section three, of the constitution, submitting the question: "Shall there be a convention to revise the constitution and amend the same?" and transmit a copy thereof to the sheriff of each county. Said proclamation shall designate by number the several districts in which congressional and judicial officers are to be chosen without other description. The office of senators in the state legislature shall be designated substantially as follows:

"In the senatorial districts numbered" (giving the number of each senatorial district in which a senator is to be chosen) "each one senator."

The office of representative in the state legislature shall be designated as follows:

"In the districts numbered" (giving the number of each district in which two representatives are to be chosen) "each two representatives. In all other representative districts of the state, each one representative." [36 G. A., ch. 88; C. '73, § 577; R., § 462.]

Sec. 57. **Proclamation of submission.** Whenever a proposition to amend the constitution is submitted to a vote of the electors, the governor shall include such proposed amendment in his election proclamation. [16 G. A., ch. 144, § 3.]

Sec. 1062. **Notice.** The sheriff shall give at least ten days' notice thereof, by causing a copy of such proclamation to be published in some newspaper printed in the county; or, if there be no such paper, by posting such a copy in at least five of the most public places in the county. [C. '73, § 578; R., § 463.]

Sec. 1063. **Of special election.** A similar proclamation shall be issued before any special election ordered by the governor, designating the time at which such special election shall be held; and the sheriff of each county in which such election is to be held shall give notice thereof, as provided in the last section. [C. '73, § 579; R., § 464.]

Sec. 1059. **When officer to be chosen.** At the general election next preceding the expiration of the term of any officer his successor shall be elected. [C. '73, § 575; R., § 461.]

Sec. 1060. **Term of office.** The term of office of all officers chosen at a general election for a full term shall commence on the second secular day of January next thereafter, except when otherwise provided by the constitution or by statute; that of an officer chosen to fill a vacancy shall commence as soon as he has qualified therefor. [33 G. A., ch. 68, § 1; 31 G. A., ch. 37, § 1; 16 G. A., ch. 72; C. '73, § 576; R., § 462.]

See Const., Art. IV, § 15.

Sec. 1060-a. **Acts in conflict repealed.** All parts of acts in conflict with this act are hereby repealed. [33 G. A., ch. 68, § 2.]

Sec. 1065. **State officers.** The governor, lieutenant governor, secretary of state, auditor of state, treasurer of state and attorney general shall be chosen at the general election in each even-numbered year and their terms of office shall be for two years. [35 G. A., ch. 103, § 9; 31 G. A., ch. 36, § 3.]

As to governor and lieutenant governor, see Const., Art. IV, § 15.
As to secretary, auditor and treasurer, see Const., Art. IV, § 22.
As to attorney general, see Const., Art. V, § 12.

Sec. 1066. **Judges of the supreme court.** Two judges of the supreme court shall be chosen at the general election in the year nineteen hundred six and two shall be chosen at each general election thereafter, whose terms of office shall continue for six years. Of the judges whose terms of office first expire, the senior in time of service shall be chief justice for one year, and, if there be but two of them, the junior for one year, and so on in rotation. If two or more are equal in time of service, then the right to the position and the order in which they serve shall be determined by seniority in age. And at the last term in each year, the supreme court shall determine and enter of record, who, under these rules, shall be chief justice for the year next ensuing; and at the session of the supreme court next preceding the commencement of the first of the said two years, the supreme court shall cause a record to be made as to who shall be the chief justice for the year next ensuing. [35 G. A., ch. 22, § 4; 31 G. A., ch. 36, § 4; 26 G. A., ch. 72; 25 G. A., ch. 69, § 2; 16 G. A., ch. 7, § 2; C. '73, § 582; R., § 467.]

See Const., Art. V, §§ 3, 11.

Chapter 318, Laws of the Thirty-seventh General Assembly.

Superintendent of Public Instruction.

AN ACT to make the office of state superintendent of public instruction elective, repealing section twenty-six hundred twenty-seven-a (2627-a), supplement to the code, 1913, and providing for the filling of said office until the next general election.

Be It Enacted by the General Assembly of the State of Iowa:

Section 1. **Office made elective.** That the office of superintendent of public instruction is hereby made elective, and the election of said officer shall be submitted to the qualified voters of Iowa at the general election of 1918 and every four years thereafter. The term of such officer so elected shall commence at the expiration of the term of the superintendent of public instruction now in office, and continue until his successor is elected and qualified.

Sec. 2. **Repeal.** Section twenty-six hundred twenty-seven-a (2627-a) supplement to the code, 1913, and all acts and parts of acts inconsistent herewith are hereby repealed.

*Sec. 193, supplement to the code, 1913, increases the number of judges from six to seven.

Sec. 1068.   Railroad commissioners—election and term.   At the general election in the year nineteen hundred six, and every four years thereafter, there shall be elected two railroad commissioners, whose term of office shall be for a period of four years; and at the general election in the year nineteen hundred eight, and every four years thereafter, there shall be elected one railroad commissioner, whose term of office shall be for a period of four years; and the present incumbents of the office of railroad commissioner shall continue in office until their successors are elected and qualified, as in this act provided.   [31 G. A., ch. 38; 22 G. A., ch. 69, § 2; 17 G. A., ch. 77, § 2.]

Sec. 1069.   Judges of district court.   The judges of the d'strict court shall be elected in each judicial district at a general election, and shall hold office for four years, except when elected to fill a vacancy, in which case it shall be only for the unexpired term.   [21 G. A., ch. 134, § 4.]

Sec. 1071.   Senators.   Senators in the general assembly, to succeed those whose terms are about to expire, shall be elected in the respective senatorial districts in each even-numbered year, and shall hold office for the term of four years.   [31 G. A., ch. 36, § 6; C. '73, § 588; R., § 471; C. '51, § 239.]
See Const., Art. III, § 5.

Sec. 1070.   Representatives.   Members of the house of representatives shall be elected in the respective representative districts in each even-numbered year, and hold office for the term of two years.   [31 G. A., ch. 36, § 5; C. '73, § 587; R., § 470; C. '51, § 239.]
See Const., Art. III, § 3.

Sec. 1072.   County officers—election of county superintendent of schools by convention.   There shall be elected in each county, at the general election in nineteen hundred and six, and in each even-numbered year thereafter an auditor, a treasurer, a clerk of the district court, sheriff, a recorder of deeds, a county attorney, and a coroner, who shall hold office for the term of two years or until their successors are elected and qualified.   On the first Tuesday in April in the year nineteen hundred fifteen, and each third year thereafter, and whenever a vacancy occurs in the office of county superintendent of schools, a convention shall be held at the county seat for the purpose of electing a county superintendent of schools, at which convention each school township, city, town or village independent district and each independent consolidated district in the county shall be entitled to one vote. Each such school corporation shall be represented at the convention by the president of the school board, or in his absence or inability to act, by some member of such school board, to be selected by the board. It is further provided, however, that where a congressional township is composed in whole or in part of rural independent districts that such rural independent districts shall be entitled to one vote in the convention, which vote shall be cast by such person as may be selected by the presidents of the component rural independent districts within such township at a meeting to be held at such time and place as the county auditor shall fix in the written notice hereinafter provided for. All representatives to such convention shall serve until a county superintendent is elected and qualified. Such conventions shall be called by the county auditor by mailing a written notice to the president and secretary of each school corporation at least ten days prior to the date of such convention and by the publication of such notice in the official newspapers published in the county. The county auditor shall be the secretary of such convention and shall call same to order and submit a list of the school corporations entitled to participate in such conventions. Said convention shall organize by the selection of a chairman and when so organized, shall elect a county superintendent of schools, who shall possess the qualifications required by law and shall hold the office for the term of three years and until his successor is elected and qualified. Such convention may by a majority vote select a committee consisting of five members whose duty shall be to investigate the various candidates for the office of county superintendent and report to said convention at a subsequent day to which the convention may adjourn; or by a three-fourths vote of such convention, said committee may be authorized to elect a county superintendent and file its election with the county auditor, and said person shall be deemed duly elected to such office.

There shall also be held one of such conventions on the first Monday of April, 1919, at which there shall be elected six persons outside the membership of such convention, who with the county superintendent, ex officio, shall constitute the county board of education. Such persons shall be reputable citizens of the county, of good educational qualifications and whose term of office shall begin the first day of May, 1919, and continue until their successors are selected and qualified. Three of whom shall be elected for the term of two years and three for the term of five years, and thereafter beginning with the regular convention in 1921, three members shall be elected every three years for the term of six years, and until their successors are selected and qualified. All persons elected or appointed on said board shall qualify on or before ten days following their election or appointment, and at the time of their election or appointment must be citizens of the United States, over twenty-one years of age, and residents of the state for a period of six months, and the county sixty days, prior to their election or appointment, and the members of said board may be of either sex, and not more than one member, other than the county superintendent, shall be from the same school corporation. Vacancies in said board to be filled by the board until the next regular convention, when such convention shall fill all vacancies, provided, however, if the members of said board be reduced below a quorum a convention shall be called as provided by law, to fill vacancies. A majority of said board shall constitute a quorum for the transaction of business. The members of said board shall take an oath of office as provided by law for all county officers. The members of said board, except the county superintendent, shall serve without pay, but shall be allowed their actual necessary expenses in performing their duties not to exceed forty dollars each, annually, to be audited by the board of supervisors and paid out of the general fund. Meetings of said board shall be held on the second Monday of August and February in each year at the office of the county superintendent, and other meetings on call of the county superintendent, or on written request of any three members filed with the county superintendent. Said board shall perform al' duties prescribed by law for the county board of education, and upon all matters referred to them by him shall act as an advisory board to the county superintendent, and shall cooperate with him in formulating plans and regulations for the advancement and welfare of the schools under his supervision.

A majority of representatives herein provided shall constitute a quorum, such representatives to receive ten cents per mile one way for the distance necessarily traveled in attending such convention, to be paid from the county treasury. [38 G. A., ch. 56, § 2; 35 G. A., ch. 107, § 1; 34 G. A., ch. 24, § 1; 31 G. A., ch. 39; 23 G. A., ch. 37, § 2; 21 G. A., ch. 73, § 1; C. '73, § 589; R., §§ 224, 472-3; C. '51, § 96.]

(Women are by § 2748 made eligible to school offices and by § 493 to the office of county recorder.)

Sec. 411. **Members of county board of supervisors—term of office.** At the general election in the year nineteen hundred six there shall be elected for a term of two years, members of the county board of supervisors to succeed those whose terms were extended one year by the biennial election amendment. At the general election in the year nineteen hundred six, and biennially thereafter, there shall be elected members of the board of supervisors for a term of three years to succeed those whose terms of office will expire on the second secular day in January following said election; there shall also be elected members for a term of three years to succeed those whose terms will expire on the second secular day in January one year later than the aforesaid date. It shall be specified on the ballot when each shall begin his term of office. No member shall be elected who is a resident of the same township with either of the members holding over (but a member-elect may be a resident of the same township as the member he is elected to succeed), except that, in counties having five or seven supervisors, and having therein a township embracing an entire city of thirty-five thousand inhabitants or over, he may be a resident of the same township; and in no case shall there be more than two supervisors from such township. [36 G. A., ch. 175, § 1; 31 G. A., ch. 12, § 2; C. '73, § 295.]

Sec. 1074. **Township trustees—election—term.** At the general election in the year nineteen hundred eighteen, there shall be elected in each township one trustee whose term of office shall be for a period of two years, and one trustee whose term of office shall be for a period of three years, and one trustee whose term of office shall be for a period of four years.

At the general election in the year nineteen hundred twenty, and biennially thereafter, there shall be elected a township trustee for a term of three years to succeed the one whose term will expire on the second secular day in January following said election: there shall also be elected a township trustee for a term of three years to succeed the one whose term expires on the second secular day of January one year later than the aforesaid date. It shall be specified on the ballot when each shall begin his term. [37 G. A., ch. 204; 31 G. A., ch. 37, § 2; 17 G. A., ch. 12, §§ 1, 2; C. '73, § 591; R., § 475.]

Sec. 1073. **Justices and constables.** In all townships, except such as are included in the territorial limits of municipal courts, there shall be elected by the voters at the general election, two justices of the peace and two constables, who shall hold office two years and be county officers. [36 G. A., ch. 106, § 51; 25 G. A., ch. 74, § 4; C. '73, §§ 389, 590, 592-3; R., §§ 443, 726, 474, 477-8; C. '51, § 221, 243.]

Sec. 1075. **Township clerk—assessor.** At the general election in each even-numbered year, there shall be elected in each civil township one township clerk, and, where not otherwise provided, one assessor, to be elected by the voters of such district, who shall hold their offices for the term of two years. [29 G. A., ch. 53, § 1; 18 G. A., ch. 161, § 1; C. '73, § 591; R., § 475.]

The offices of township trustee and clerk are abolished in some cases where the township constitutes a city or town. See §§ 560, 562.

As to method of voting for assessor, see § 1130.

Sec. 1074-a. **In new townships—special election.** At any time when a new township has been created in a year in which no general election is held by law, the county board of supervisors of the county affected shall call a special election for the election of three trustees and other township officers of the new township, which officers shall continue in office until their successors are elected and qualified. [32 G. A., ch. 49.]

Sec. 565. **Assessor where city included.** In each even-numbered year there shall be elected in each township, a part of which is included within the corporate limits of any city or town, by the voters of such township residing without the corporate limits of such city or town, one assessor who shall be a resident of said territory outside of said city or town. [33 G. A., ch. 37; 19 G. A., ch. 110; 18 G. A., ch. 201, § 1; 16 G. A., ch. 6; C. '73, § 390.]

DIVISION II.

ELECTIONS AND OFFICERS: CITIES AND TOWNS.

Section 642. Regular elections. The regular municipal elections in cities and towns shall be held annually or biennially, as hereafter provided, on the last Monday in March. The voting places shall be fixed by the council, one polling place for each precinct, and the election shall be conducted in the manner provided by law for general elections. Each qualified elector may vote thereat who is a resident of the city or town, and, at the time, has been ten days a resident of the precinct in which he offers to vote. [23 G. A., ch. 1, § 5; C. '73, § 501.]

For date of municipal primary elections, see § 1087-a34, post.

Sec. 643. Officers to be residents. Every mayor, councilman-at-large, town councilman and officer elected by the whole electorate of the city or town, or by its council, or appointed by the council, mayor or other officer of any city or town, shall be a resident and qualified elector of the city in which he shall be elected, and shall reside within the limits of said city during his term of office. [21 G. A., ch. 141, § 1; 19 G. A., ch. 25; 17 G. A., chs. 9, 14; 16 G. A., ch. 58; C. '73, §§ 511, 518, 521; R., §§ 1091, 1093.]

Sec. 644. Qualifications of officers. Every councilman and other officer elected by any ward or district of any city or town shall be a qualified elector of said city or town, residing within the limits of the ward or district in which he shall be elected, and shall reside within the limits of said ward or district during the term of his office. [19 G. A., ch. 25; 17 G. A., ch. 14; C. '73, § 521; R., § 1093.]

Sec. 645. Council—how composed. City and town councils shall be composed as follows: In cities, two councilmen at large and one councilman from each ward; in towns, five councilmen at large. [32 G. A., ch. 26, § 2; 29 G. A., ch. 29, § 2; 19 G. A., ch. 25; 18 G. A., ch. 120; 17 G. A., chs. 9, 14; C. '73, §§ 511, 521, 531; R., §§ 1081, 1093.]

Sec. 646. Election of councilmen—terms of office. On the organization of a city or town or on its reorganization after the change of its class, or at the first regular municipal election hereafter, a council shall be elected as follows, except that in those cities of the second class that elect a mayor in odd-

numbered years, the term of those councilmen and officers ex-
piring in nineteen hundred and eight is extended one year; in
those cities of the second class that elect a mayor in even-numbered years, the term of those councilmen and officers expir-
ing in nineteen hundred and nine is extended one year; and at
the municipal election at which a mayor is elected in nineteen
hundred and nine or nineteen hundred ten, as the case may be,
the council shall be elected in accordance with the provisions
of this act: By the election of two councilmen at large, but
if any city embraces within its limits the whole or part of two
or more townships, two of which contain one thousand or more
electors, only one of the councilmen at large shall be chosen
from any one township. There shall also be elected at the
same time one councilman from each ward, who shall be chosen
by the electors residing within the limits thereof. Thereafter,
the successors of such councilmen at large and ward councilmen and officers shall be chosen at the regular biennial elections and shall hold office for two years. In towns in which a
mayor is elected in the even-numbered years the officers and
councilmen shall be elected under the provisions of this act in
the year nineteen hundred ten, and the councilmen and officers
to be elected in nineteen hundred and eight shall be elected for
a term of two years, and the term of councilmen and officers
whose terms expire in nineteen hundred and nine shall be extended one year. In towns in which a mayor is elected in odd-
numbered years the officers and councilmen shall be elected
under the provisions of this act in nineteen hundred eleven, and
the councilmen and officers to be elected in nineteen hundred
and eight shall be elected for a term of three years. The councilmen and officers to be elected in nineteen hundred and nine
shall be elected for two years, and the term of councilmen and
officers whose term expires in nineteen hundred ten shall be
extended one year. All town officers[1] elected in nineteen hundred ten or nineteen hundred eleven, as the case may be, and
thereafter under the provisions of this act, shall be elected for
the term of two years. [32 G. A., ch. 26, § 3; 19 G. A., ch. 25;
17 G. A.; chs. 9, 14; C. '73, §§ 511, 521; R., § 1093.]

Sec. 647. **Elective officers in cities of first class.** In all
cities of the first class there shall be elected biennially a mayor,
solicitor, treasurer, auditor, city engineer, assessor, and in

---

[1"offices" in session laws.]

cities where there is no superior court, a police judge. [32 G. A., ch. 26, § 4; 19 G. A., ch. 110; 18 G. A., ch. 201, § 1; 17 G. A., ch. 20; 16 G. A., chs. 6, 33; C. '73, §§ 390, 535; R., § 1106.]

Sec. 648. Elective officers in cities of second class. In cities of the second class there shall be elected biennially a mayor, treasurer and assessor. [35 G. A., ch. 54, § 1; 32 G. A., ch. 26, § 5; 21 G. A., ch. 141; 19 G. A., ch. 110; 16 G. A., ch. 6; C. '73, §§ 390, 517, 532; R., §§ 1090, 1103.]

Sec. 649. Elective officers in towns. In towns there shall be elected, biennially, a mayor, treasurer and assessor. [32 G. A., ch. 26, § 6; 19 G. A., ch. 110; 17 G. A., ch. 9; 16 G. A., ch. 6; C. '73, §§ 390, 511, 514; R., §§ 1081, 1084.]

Sec. 650. Terms of office—assessor. Each officer named in this chapter shall hold his office until his successor is elected and qualified; but the term of office of the assessor shall commence on the first day of January, next ensuing his election. [19 G. A., ch. 110; 18 G. A., ch. 201, § 1; 16 G. A., chs. 3, 33; C. '73, § 390.]

DIVISION III.

ELECTIONS AND OFFICERS: CITIES UNDER SPECIAL CHARTER.

Section 936. Elections. All elections held in such cities shall be governed by the general election laws.

Sec. 937. Council—vacancies. In any such city having a population of twenty thousand or more, as shown by the last state or national census, the council shall consist of two aldermen at large, and one alderman from each ward. At the first annual city election after the taking effect of this code, there shall be elected two aldermen at large, and one alderman from each ward. Thereafter the successors of such aldermen shall be elected biennially. The aldermen in office at the time of taking effect of this code shall continue in office only until the election and qualification of the aldermen herein provided for. The mayor shall be the presiding officer of the council, with the right to vote only in case of a tie. Vacancies, now existing or hereafter occurring, in the office of alderman, shall be filled by special election, unless such vacancy shall have occurred less than sixty days prior to a regular city election. Such special election shall be called by a proclamation of the mayor, giving at least ten days' notice of such election, designating the time and polling places therefor and the vacancy to be filled thereat. Notice of such election shall be published in at least one newspaper printed and published in said city and in two, if there be such number, for a period of ten days prior to such election. Notice of such election shall be posted at or near the polling places designated for said election for a similar length of time. The election board at any such special election shall be the same as at the last preceding city election. In case of vacancies happening therein the mayor shall make appointments to fill the same, such appointee to be a member of the same political party or organization as the member filling such position before the vacancy. (The city clerk shall, on notice from the mayor cause ballots to be prepared for such election as provided by law; or, in the event of his refusal or inability to act, the mayor shall cause such ballots to be prepared.) Nominations of candidates for such vacant office may be made by caucus or convention, as provided in section one thousand ninety-eight of the code; or, in the event such nomination be not made by such caucus or convention, within five days prior to the day fixed for holding such election, then the regular executive or city central committee, of any party qualified to nominate by caucus or convention, may make such nomination. [38 G. A., ch. 185, § 1; 36 G. A., ch. 2, § 1; 35 G. A., ch. 94, § 1.]

Sec. 937-a. Vacancies—when filled by council. In the event that such vacancy shall have occurred less than sixty days prior to a regular city election, then the vacancy so existing shall be filled by a majority vote, of the remaining aldermen of the city council. [36 G. A., ch. 2, § 2.]

Sec. 937-b. Conflicting acts repealed. That all acts or parts of acts in so far as in conflict herewith be and the same are hereby repealed. [36 G. A., ch. 2, § 3.]

Sec. 938. Marshal—policemen. Cities under special charter shall have power to provide by ordinance for the appointment of a marshal by the mayor, or for his election by the electors thereof, or may dispense with such officer, and confer his duties upon any other officer. All policemen shall be appointed and may be removed by the mayor. [22 G. A., ch. 23, § 1; 18 G. A., ch. 24, § 1.]

Sec. 939. **Assessors.** They shall provide by ordinance for the election of one or more assessors, who shall discharge the duties usually performed by township assessors, so far as applicable, and such as may be required by ordinance. [22 G. A., ch. 27; 21 G. A., ch. 93, § 3; 16 G. A., ch. 90, §1.]

Sec. 940. **Other officers elected—terms.** They may provide by ordinance for the election, by the electors, of a marshal, recorder or clerk, treasurer, collector, auditor, attorney, and engineer; and all elective officers hereafter elected shall hold office for the term of two years, and until their successors are elected and qualified, and, when appointed, for such time as may be fixed by ordinance, not exceeding two years. [22 G. A., ch. 27; 21 G. A., ch. 93, § 3.]

Sec. 991. **Park commissioners—election—ordinance submitted—terms.** There shall be elected at the regular municipal election in each city acting under special charter, and containing a population of forty thousand or over, and all other special charter cities may by ordinance provide for the election of three park commissioners whose terms of office shall be six years, one to be elected at each regular municipal election. At the first regular municipal election after the passage hereof, three commissioners shall be elected, and shall hold their office respectively for two, four and six years, their respective terms to be decided by lot, and their successor shall be elected for the full term of six years; provided, however, that in all such cities under special charter, and containing a population of less than forty thousand, not now having park commissioners, the ordinance establishing such park commissioners shall not be in force until it has been submitted to the voters at a special or regular municipal election, and approved by a majority of the votes cast at such election; and provided further, that in all such cities under special charter containing a population of forty thousand or over, in which there already exists a board of three park commissioners whose term of office is six years, and one of the members of which board is elected every two years at each regular municipal election, the three commissioners at present holding the office of park commissioners in such cities are hereby made the commissioners in such city in accordance with the provisions of this act, and they and their successors shall have and exercise all the powers and duties of park commissioners within the provisions of this act. [34 G. A., ch. 46, §§ 1, 2; 20 G. A., ch. 151, §§ 1, 2.]

DIVISION IV.

ELECTIONS AND OFFICERS: CITIES UNDER COMMISSION FORM OF GOVERNMENT.

Section 1056-a20.   Elective officers—vacancies—terms of office. In every city having a population of twenty-five thousand and over there shall be elected at the regular biennial municipal election a mayor and four councilmen, and in every city having a population of two thousand and less than twenty-five thousand, there shall be elected at such election a mayor and two councilmen. If any vacancy occurs in any such office the remaining members of said council shall appoint a person to fill such vacancy during the balance of the unexpired term. Said officers shall be nominated and elected at large. Said officers shall qualify and their terms of office shall begin on the first Monday after their election. The terms of office of the mayor and councilmen or aldermen in such city in office at the beginning of the terms of office of the mayor and councilmen first elected under the provisions of this act shall then cease and determine, and the terms of office of all other appointive officers in force in such city, except as hereinafter provided, shall cease and determine as soon as the council shall by resolution declare. [35 G. A., ch. 102, § 1; 33 G. A., ch. 64, § 4; 32 G. A., ch. 48, § 4.]

Sec. 1056-a21.   Candidates—how nominated—primary election—ballot—canvass of vote—result published—municipal election. Candidates to be voted for at all general municipal elections at which a mayor and councilmen are to be elected under the provisions of this act shall be nominated by a primary election, and no other names shall be placed upon the general ballot except those selected in the manner hereinafter prescribed. The primary election for such nomination shall be held on the second Monday preceding the general municipal election. The judges of election appointed for the general municipal election shall be the judges of the primary election, and it shall be held at the same place, so far as possible, and the polls shall be opened and closed at the same hours, with the same clerks as are required for said general municipal election. Any person desiring to become a candidate for mayor or councilman shall, at least ten days prior to said primary election, file with the said clerk a statement of such candidacy, in substantially the following form:

STATE OF IOWA,

....County, } ss:

I (..................................) being first duly sworn, say that I reside at.................................street, city of.................................... county of.................................state of Iowa; that I am a qualified voter therein; that I am a candidate for nomination to the office of (mayor or councilman) to be voted upon at the primary election to be held on the...........Monday of.................... 19........ and I hereby request that my name be printed upon the official primary ballot for nomination by such primary election for such office.

(Signed) ....

Subscribed and sworn to (or affirmed) before me by............... ....on this...............day of...............................19.........

(Signed) ....

and shall at the same time file therewith the petition of at least twenty-five qualified voters requesting such candidacy. Each petition shall be verified by one or more persons as to the qualifications and residence, with street number, of each of the persons so signing the said petition, and the said petition shall be in substantially the following form:

PETITION ACCOMPANYING NOMINATING STATEMENT.

The undersigned, duly qualified electors of the city of............ .... and residing at the places set opposite our respective names hereto, do hereby request that the name of (name of candidate) be placed on the ballot as a candidate for nomination for (name of office) at the primary election to be held in such city on the...............Monday of............................... 19........ We further state that we know him to be a qualified elector of said city and a man of good moral character and qualified in our judgment for the duties of such office.

Name of qualified electors.   -   Number.   Street.

Immediately upon the expiration of the time of filing the statements and petitions for candidacies, the said city clerk shall cause to be published for three successive days in all the daily newspapers published in the city, in proper form, the names of the persons as they are to appear upon the primary ballot, and if there be no daily newspaper, then in two issues of any other newspapers that may be published in said city; and the said clerk shall thereupon cause the primary ballots to be printed, authenticated with a facsimile of his signature. Upon the said ballot the names of the candidates for mayor, arranged alphabetically, shall first be placed, with a square at the left of each name, and immediately below the words, "Vote for one." Following these names, likewise arranged in alphabetical order, shall appear the names of the candidates for councilmen, with a square at the left of each name, and below the names of such candidates shall appear the words "Vote for four," or "Vote for two" as the case may be. The ballots shall be printed upon plain, substantial white paper, and shall be headed:

CANDIDATES FOR NOMINATION FOR MAYOR AND COUNCILMEN OF
----------------------------------CITY AT THE PRIMARY ELECTION.
but shall have no party designation or mark whatever. The ballots shall be in substantially the following form:

(Place a cross in the square preceding the names of the parties you favor as candidates for the respective positions.)

OFFICIAL PRIMARY BALLOT.
CANDIDATES FOR NOMINATION FOR MAYOR AND COUNCILMEN OF
----------------------------------CITY AT THE PRIMARY ELECTION.

For Mayor

☐ (Name of candidate)

(Vote for one)

For Councilman

☐ (Name of candidate)

(Vote for four) or (Vote for two)

as the case may be.

Official ballot attest

(Signature)

City Clerk.

Having caused said ballots to be printed, the said city clerk shall cause to be delivered at each polling place a number of said ballots equal to twice the number of votes cast in such polling precinct at the last general municipal election for mayor. The persons who are qualified to vote at the general municipal election shall be qualified to vote at such primary election, and challenges can be made by not more than two persons, to be appointed at the time of opening the polls by the judges of election; and the law applicable to challenges at a general municipal election shall be applicable to challenges made at such primary election. Judges of election shall, immediately upon the closing of the polls, count the ballots and ascertain the number of votes cast in such precinct for each of the candidates, and make return thereof to the city clerk, upon proper blanks to be furnished by the said clerk, within six hours of the closing of the polls. On the day following the said primary election, the said city clerk shall canvass said returns so received from all the polling precincts, and shall make and publish in all the newspapers of said city, at least once, the result thereof. Said canvass by the city clerk shall be publicly made. The two candidates receiving the highest number of votes for mayor shall be the candidates, and the only candidates, whose names shall be placed upon the ballot for mayor at the next succeeding general municipal election; and in cities having a population of twenty-five thousand and over, the eight candidates receiving the highest number of votes for councilman, or all such candidates if less than eight, and in cities having a population of two thousand and less than twenty-five thousand, the four candidates receiving the highest number of votes for councilman, or all such candidates if less than four, shall be the candidates, and the only candidates, whose names shall be placed upon the ballot for councilman at such municipal election. All electors of cities under this act who by the laws governing cities of the first and second class and cities acting under special charter would be entitled to vote for the election of officers at any general municipal election in such cities, shall be qualified to vote at all elections under this act; and the ballot at such general municipal election shall be in the same general form as for such primary election, so far as applicable; and in all elections in such city, the election precinct, voting places, method of conducting election, canvassing the vote and announcing the results shall be the same as by law provided for election of officers in such cities, so far as the same are applicable and not inconsistent with the provisions of this act. [35 G. A., ch. 102, § 1; 33 G. A., ch. 64, § 5; 32 G. A., ch. 48, § 5.]

Sec. 1056-a22. Services for hire—penalty. Any person who shall agree to perform any services in the interest of any candidate for any office provided in this act, in consideration of any money or other valuable thing for such services performed in the interest of any candidate, shall be punished by a fine not exceeding three hundred dollars, or be imprisoned in the county jail not exceeding thirty days. [32 G. A., ch. 48, § 5-a.]

Sec. 1056-a23. Bribery and illegal voting—penalty. Any person offering to give a bribe, either in money or other consideration, to any elector for the purpose of influencing his vote at any election provided in this act, or any elector entitled to vote at any such election receiving and accepting such bribe or other consideration; any person making false answer to any of the provisions of this act relative to his qualifications to vote at said election; any person wilfully voting or offering to vote at such election who has not been a resident of this state for six months next preceding said election, or who is not twenty-one years of age, or is not a citizen of the United States, or knowing himself not to be a qualified elector of such precinct where he offers to vote; any person knowingly procuring, aiding or abetting any violation hereof shall be deemed guilty of a misdemeanor and upon conviction shall be fined a sum not less than one hundred dollars, nor more than five hundred dollars, and be imprisoned in the county jail not less than ten nor more than ninety days. [32 G. A., ch. 48, § 5-b.]

Sec. 1056-a31. Officers and employes—what prohibited.* Any officer or employe of such city who, by solicitation or otherwise, shall exert his influence directly or indirectly to influence other officers or employes of such city to adopt his political views or to favor any particular person or candidate for office, or who shall in any manner contribute money, labor, or other valuable thing to any person for election purposes. shall be guilty of a misdemeanor and upon conviction shall be punished by a fine not exceeding three hundred dollars or by imprisonment in the county jail not exceeding thirty days. [32 G. A., ch. 48, § 13.]

Sec. 1056-a32. Civil service commissioners—duties—powers of council.*

---

*Portions of this section, not applicable to elections, are omitted.

(d1) *Campaign contributions prohibited — penalty.* No member of the fire or police department in any such city shall directly or indirectly contribute any money or anything of value to any candidate for nomination or election to any office or to any campaign or political committee. Any person violating any of the provisions of this section shall be deemed guilty of a misdemeanor and upon conviction shall pay a fine of not less than twenty-five dollars nor more than one hundred dollars, or be imprisoned in the county jail not to exceed thirty days. [34 G. A., ch. 54, § 5.]

(f) *Officers and employes affected.** It shall be unlawful for any candidate for office, or any officer in any such city, directly or indirectly, to give or promise any person or persons any office, position, employment, benefit, or anything of value, for the purpose of influencing or obtaining the political support, aid or vote of any person or persons. Every elective officer in any such city shall, within thirty days after qualifying, file with the city clerk, and publish at least once in a daily newspaper of general circulation, his sworn statement of all his election and campaign expenses, and by whom such funds were contributed. Any violation of the provisions of this section shall be a misdemeanor and be a ground for removal from office. [35 G. A., ch. 102, § 1; 33 G. A., ch. 64, § 10; 32 G. A., ch. 48, § 14.]

Sec. 1056-a36. **Removal of elective officers—procedure—statement of candidacy—election of successors.** The holder of any elective office may be removed at any time by the electors qualified to vote for a successor of such incumbent. The procedure to effect the removal of an incumbent of an elective office shall be as follows: A petition signed by electors entitled to vote for a successor to the incumbent sought to be removed, equal in number to at least twenty-five per centum of the entire vote for all candidates for the office of mayor cast at the last preceding general municipal election, demanding an election of a successor of the person sought to be removed, shall be filed with the city clerk, which petition shall contain a general statement of the grounds for which the removal is sought. The signatures to the petition need not all be appended to one paper, but each signer shall add to his signature his place of residence, giving the street and number. One of the

*Portions of this section, not applicable to elections, are omitted.

signers of each such paper shall make oath before an officer competent to administer oaths that the statements therein made are true as he believes, and that each signature to the paper appended is the genuine signature of the person whose name it purports to be. Within ten days from the date of filing such petition the city clerk shall examine and from the voters' register ascertain whether or not said petition is signed by the requisite number of qualified electors, and, if necessary, the council shall allow him extra help for that purpose; and he shall attach to said petition his certificate, showing the result of said examination. If by the clerk's certificate the petition is shown to be insufficient, it may be amended within ten days from the date of said certificate. The clerk shall, within ten days after such amendment, make like examination of the amended petition, and if his certificate shall show the same to be insufficient, it shall be returned to the person filing the same; without prejudice, however, to the filing of a new petition to the same effect. If the petition shall be deemed to be sufficient, the clerk shall submit the same to the council without delay. If the petition shall be found to be sufficient, the council shall order and fix a date for holding the said election, not less than thirty days or more than forty days from the date of the clerk's certificate to the council that a sufficient petition is filed. The council shall make or cause to be made publication of notice and all arrangements for holding such election, and the same shall be conducted, returned and the result thereof declared, in all respects as are other city elections. So far as applicable, except as otherwise herein provided, nominations hereunder shall be made without the intervention of a primary election by filing with the clerk at least ten days prior to said special election, a statement of candidacy accompanied by a petition signed by electors entitled to vote at said special election equal in number to at least ten per centum of the entire vote for all candidates for the office of mayor at the last preceding general municipal election, which said statement of candidacy and petition shall be substantially in the form set out in section ten hundred fifty-six-a twenty-one, of the supplement to the code, 1907, so far as the same is applicable, substituting the word "special" for the word "primary" in such statement and petition, and stating therein that such person is a candidate for election instead of nomination.

The ballot for such special election shall be in substantially the following form:

OFFICIAL BALLOT.

Special election for the balance of the unexpired term

of .... as ....

FOR...•

(Vote for one only)

(Names of Candidates)

☐ ....

☐ ....

Name of present incumbent.

Official ballot attest:

(Signature)...

City Clerk.

The successor of any officer so removed shall hold office during the unexpired term of his predecessor. Any person sought to be removed may be a candidate to succeed himself, and unless he requests otherwise in writing, the clerk shall place his name on the official ballot without nomination. In any such removal election, the candidate receiving the highest number of votes shall be declared elected. At such election if some other person than the incumbent receives the highest number of votes, the incumbent shall thereupon be deemed removed from the office upon qualification of his successor. In case the party who receives the highest number of votes should fail to qualify within ten days after receiving notification of election, the office shall be deemed vacant. If the incumbent receives the highest number of votes, he shall continue in office. The said method of removal shall be cumulative and additional to the methods heretofore provided by law. [33 G. A., ch. 65, § 1; 32 G. A., ch. 48, § 18.]

DIVISION V.

ELECTIONS AND OFFICERS: CITIES UNDER CITY MANAGER PLAN.

Section 1056-b3. Tenure of office of councilmen, other officers and employes. The councilmen elected at the special election called by the mayor, after the adoption of the form of government contemplated by this act, shall qualify, and their terms of office shall begin on the first Monday after their election, and they shall hold office until the next regular biennial municipal election, and until their successors are elected and qualified. At the first regular biennial election, after the organization of any city or town, under the provisions of this act, in all such cities and towns where three councilmen are to be elected, one councilman shall be elected for the term of two years, and two for the term of three years. When four councilmen are to be elected, as provided in section two hereof, one shall be elected from each township for the term of two years, and one from each township for the term of three years, and in cities where five councilmen are to be elected, two shall be elected for two years, and three for three years. At the next regular biennial municipal election, and biennially thereafter, there shall be elected, a member or members of the council for the term of three years to succeed those whose terms of office will expire the first Monday in April, following such election, and there shall also be elected at such regular biennial municipal election, a member or members of the council for a term of three years to succeed those whose terms will expire one year after the first Monday in April following such election.

The time when each candidate for councilman shall begin his term of office shall be specified under his name on the ballot, and all petitions for nomination of members of the council, to be voted for at such regular biennial municipal election, shall specify the length of the term of office for which the candidate seeks nomination. The terms of office of the mayor and councilmen or aldermen of any city or incorporated town, adopting the form of government contemplated by this act, in office at the beginning of the terms of office of the councilmen first elected, under the provisions hereof, shall then cease and determine, and except the members of the library board, whose terms of office shall continue as now provided by law, the terms of office of all other officers including park commissioners, members of the board of public works, and waterworks trustees, whether elected or appointed, and of all employes of such city or incorporated town, shall be subject to the action of the council or manager, as herein provided. Except the members of the library board, the council shall have power to determine the tenure of office of any officer or the term of employment of any employe that it is authorized to appoint or employ, and to declare any such office vacant, or to discharge any such employe with or without cause, as it may deem advisable, and the manager shall have power to determine the tenure of office of any officer or the term of employment of any employe that he is authorized to appoint or employ, and to declare any such office vacant, or to discharge any such employe with or without cause, as he may deem advisable. [36 G. A., ch. 180, § 4.]

Sec. 1056-b4. **Councilmen to be nominated by petition—election—form of ballot.** Candidates for councilmen, to be voted for under the provisions of this act, shall be nominated by petition, filed with the city or town clerk, ten days before the day of election, and no name shall be placed upon the ballot, except the names of candidates nominated by such petition. The petition for the nomination of councilmen shall be signed by at least ten electors of the city or town, for every one thousand inhabitants of such city or town, as shown by the last previous federal or state census, and no petitioner shall sign any petition or petitions for more candidates than are to be elected in the city or town in which such petition is filed. No person shall be deemed nominated for the office of councilman, unless the petition for his nomination shall have been signed as herein required. The petition for the nomination of councilmen shall be substantially in the following form:

"The undersigned, duly qualified electors of (here insert the name of the city or town), and residing at the place set opposite our respective names, hereby nominate (name of candidate), as candidate for the office of councilman, of the (name of city or town), and request that his name be placed upon the official ballot of said city (or town), at the municipal election to be held therein, on the............Monday of......................., 19......... We further state that we know the said (name of candidate) to be a qualified elector of said city (or town), a man of good moral character, and in our judgment, qualified for the duties of councilman.

Name of electors.   Residence.   Street and number.

In cities where the residences are numbered, the street and number of the residence of each elector, signing such petition, shall be written on the petition immediately after the name of the elector, and no name upon any such petition shall be counted unless the street and number of the residence of the person signing the same appear thereon, as herein provided. Petitions for nomination of councilmen, filed with the city or town clerk, shall, within two days after the expiration of the time within which such petitions may be filed, be canvassed by the city or town council, as the case may be, and the names of all persons who shall have been nominated by such petitions, shall, by the clerk, be placed upon the official ballot of the city or town, of the municipal election for which such nominations are made. The names of the candidates shall be arranged upon the ballot in the manner provided by section ten hundred eighty-seven-a thirteen, supplement to the code, 1913, as nearly as may be, with a square at the left of each name, and below the names of each of such candidates, shall appear the words, vote for (here insert the number of councilmen to be elected) as the case may be. The ballots shall be printed upon plain, substantial white paper, through which the printing or writing cannot be read, and shall be headed, "Candidates for councilmen of (name of city or town), at the general (or special) municipal election of 19.........." The candidates upon the ballot shall be voted for by placing a cross in the square preceding the name of the candidate for whom the vote is cast. [37 G. A., ch. 15; 36 G. A., ch. 180, § 5.]

Sec. 1056-b5. Ballots—clerk to prepare—number—judges —canvass of returns. The city or town clerk shall cause the ballots to be prepared and printed as herein specified, and shall deliver, or cause to be delivered, at every polling precinct in the city or town, a number of ballots equal to twice the number of votes cast at such precinct at the last general municipal election. The city or town council shall appoint the judges and clerks of the election. The election shall be conducted, the vote canvassed, and the certified return thereof made by the judges of such election as provided by law. The returns from the voting precincts shall be canvassed, the result declared by the council, and clerk, on the day after the election, and notice of the result given at the time and in the manner provided by statute. [36 G. A., ch. 180, § 6.]

Sec. 1056-b6. Election laws applicable. All of the provisions of section ten hundred fifty-six-a twenty-two, and ten hundred fifty-six-a twenty-three, supplement to the code, 1913, shall apply to elections held under the provisions of this act, and any person violating any of the provisions of either of said sections shall, upon conviction thereof, be punished as therein provided. [36 G. A., ch. 180, § 7.]

Sec. 1056-b11. **Statutes made applicable.** All of the provisions of section ten hundred fifty-six-a thirty-one, supplement to the code, 1913, shall apply to all officers and employees elected or appointed in any city or town, organized under this act, as fully as though the provisions of such section were incorporated and repeated herein. [36 G. A., ch. 180, § 12.]

Sec. 1056-b20. **Manager not to influence election—penalty.** The manager shall take no part in any election held for the purpose of electing councilmen, except that he may attend at the polls and cast his vote, if he is a qualified elector of the city or town, and any attempt upon his part to procure the election of any person as councilman, or to induce any elector to vote for any person for councilman, or any solicitation by such manager, of any elector to vote for any person or persons, for the office of councilman, shall be a misdemeanor, and upon conviction thereof, he shall be punished as provided by section nineteen hundred six of the code, and in addition to such punishment, he may be removed from office, under the provisions of chapter eight, title six, supplement to the code, 1913. [36 G. A., ch. 180, § 21.]

DIVISION VI.

VACANCIES IN OFFICE.

Section 1277. **Officers to fill vacancies.** Officers elected to fill vacancies, either at a special or general election, shall hold for the unexpired portion of the term, and until a successor is elected and qualified, unless otherwise provided by law. [C. '73, § 513; R., § 1083.]

Sec. 1278. **Officers—Vacancies.** If a vacancy occurs in an elective office in a city, town or township ten days, or a county office fifteen days, or any other office thirty days, prior to a general election, it shall be filled at such election, unless previously filled at a special election. [19 G. A., ch. 124, § 2; C. '73, §§ 530, 789, 794-5; R., §§ 672, 1101; C. '51, §§ 35, 431-5.]

Sec. 1279. **Election to Fill Vacancies.** A special election to fill a vacancy shall be held for a representative in congress, or senator or representative in the general assembly, when the body in which such vacancy exists is in session, or will convene prior to the next general election, and the governor shall order such special election at the earliest practicable time, giving ten days' notice thereof. [C. '73, § 789; R., § 672; C. '51, §§ 35, 431-5.]

DIVISION VII.
NOMINATIONS BY PRIMARY ELECTION.

Section 1087-a2. Primary election defined. The term "primary election" as used in this act shall be construed to apply to an election by the members of the various political parties for the purpose of placing in nomination candidates for public office, for selecting delegates to conventions, and for the selection of party committeemen. [32 G. A., ch. 51, § 2.]

Sec. 1087-a3. **Political party defined.** The title "political party" shall mean a party which, at the last preceding general election, cast for its candidate for governor at least two per centum of the total vote cast at said election, provided that such other political organizations as may, under sections ten hundred ninety-eight and ten hundred ninety-nine of the code, nominate and certify candidates and have their names placed upon the ballot for the November election, shall have the right so to do in the manner and under the conditions therein prescribed. [32 G. A., ch. 51, § 3.]

Sec. 1087-a1. **Primary elections authorized — offices affected.** That from and after the passage of this act the candidates of political parties for all offices which under the law are filled by the direct vote of the voters of this state at the general election in November, (except candidates for the office of judge of the supreme, district and superior courts*), for the office of senator in the congress of the United States, and for the office of elector of the president and vice president of the United States, shall be nominated by a primary election, and delegates to the county conventions of said political parties or organizations and party county committeemen shall be elected

---

*See pp. 57-60 for provisions relative to nomination and election of judges

at said primary election, at the times and in the manner hereinafter provided. The provisions of chapters three and four, title six, and chapter eight, title twenty-four, of the code, shall apply so far as applicable to all such primary elections, the same as general elections, except as hereinafter provided. [33 G. A., ch. 69, § 1; 32 G. A., ch. 51, §1.]

Sec. 1087-c. United States senators—nomination and election. In the year preceding the expiration of the term of office of United States senator, or in case of a vacancy in said office, candidates for the different parties for United States senator shall be nominated as provided by law and the United States senator or senators as the case may be shall be elected at the general election in the same manner as state officers are elected. [38 G. A., ch. 86, §9; 35 G. A., ch. 105, §1.]

Chapter 401, Laws of the Thirty-seventh General Assembly, as amended by Chapter 215, Acts of the Thirty-eighth General Assembly.

United States Senators.

AN ACT to repeal the law concerning the selection of senators in the congress of the United States by joint conventions of the general assembly, and providing for filling vacancies in the places of the senators in the congress of the United States by election and temporary appointment by the governor.

Be It Enacted by the General Assembly of the State of Iowa:

Section 1. Amendatory clause. Section thirty (30) of the code is hereby amended by striking therefrom the following: "Joint conventions for the purpose of electing a senator in the congress of the United States, and".

Sec. 2. Vacancies—when governor may fill. If the offices of the senators in the congress of the United States, or either of them, shall become vacant when the senate is in session or will convene prior to the next general election, the governor may make temporary appointment until the people fill the vacancy at the next succeeding general election, as provided by section ten hundred eighty-seven-c (1087-c), supplement to the code, 1913.

Sec. 1087-a4. When held. The primary election herein provided for shall consist of an election by all political parties and

shall be held at the usual voting places of the several precincts
on the first Monday in June, in the year nineteen hundred
twelve, and biennially thereafter, for the nomination of candidates for such offices as are to be filled at the general election
in November next ensuing (except candidates for the office of
judge of the supreme, district and superior courts*), for senator in the congress of the United States in the next year preceding the filling of that office by the general assembly,† and
for the electors of the president and vice president of the
United States, in the year in which a president and vice president are to be elected. [34 G. A., ch. 58, § 1; 32 G. A., ch. 51,
§ 4.]

Sec. 1087-a11. Blank nomination papers. The secretary of
state shall cause to be printed and keep on hand a sufficient
quantity of nomination paper blanks in form as provided for in
this act and shall furnish the same on application to any qualified elector in the state desiring to petition for the nomination
of any candidate, or to a person who intends to be a candidate,
for any office whose nomination paper is required to be filed in
his office; and the county auditor of each county shall likewise
cause to be printed and keep on hand a sufficient quantity of
such nomination paper blanks and furnish the same on application to any qualified elector in his county desiring to petition
for the nomination of any candidate, or to a person who intends
to be a candidate, for any office whose nomination paper is required to be filed in his office. [32 G. A., ch. 51, § 11.]

Sec. 1087-a10. Nomination papers—candidates — affidavit.
No candidate for an elective county office shall have his name
printed upon the official primary ballot of his party unless at
least thirty days prior to the day fixed for holding the primary
election a nomination paper shall have been filed in his behalf
in the office of the county auditor; and no candidate for nomination for an elective state office, or for representative in the
congress of the United States, or member of the general assembly, shall have his name printed upon the official primary ballot
of his party unless at least forty days prior to such primary
election a nomination paper shall have been filed in his behalf
in the office of the secretary of state; and no member of a political party desiring or intending to be a candidate for the office

*See pp. 57-60 for provisions relative to nomination and election of judges.
†See sec. 1087-c, p. 29. for provisions relative to nomination and election
of United States senator.

of senator in the congress of the United States, or a candidate for the office of elector of the president and vice president of the United States, shall have his name printed upon the official primary ballot of his party in any election precinct unless at least forty days prior to such primary election a nomination paper shall have been filed in his behalf in the office of the secretary of state. A candidate for an office to be filled by the voters of any subdivision of a county, or a candidate for party committeeman, shall not be required to file any nomination paper or papers. All nomination papers shall be in substantially the following form:

"I, the undersigned, a qualified elector of..
county, and state of Iowa, and a member of the.................................
party, hereby nominate...of...........................
county, state of Iowa, who has affiliated with and is a member of the
....party, as a candidate for the office of
.................................to be voted for at the primary election to be
held in June, 19......,"

and shall consist of sheets of uniform size about eight and one-half by thirteen inches. No signatures shall be counted unless they are on sheets each having such form written or printed at the top thereof. Each signer of a nomination paper shall sign but one such nomination paper for the same office, except where more than one officer is to be elected to the same office, in which case he may sign as many nomination papers as there are officers to be elected, and only one candidate shall be petitioned for or nominated in the same nomination paper. Each signer of a nomination paper shall add his residence with street and number, if any, and the date of signing. For all nominations, all signers of each separate part of a nomination paper shall reside in the same county. When more than one sheet is used for any nomination paper, the sheets shall be laid one upon the other and neatly, evenly, and securely fastened together before filing, and shall be considered as one nomination paper only. A nomination paper, when filed, shall not be withdrawn nor added to, nor any signature thereon revoked. The affidavit of a qualified elector shall be appended to each such nomination paper, or papers, if more than one for any candidate, stating that he is personally acquainted with all the persons who have signed the same; that he knows them to be electors of that county and believes them to be affiliated with the party named therein; that he knows that they signed the same with full knowledge of the contents thereof; that their respective residences are truly stated therein; and that each signer signed the same on the date stated opposite his name, but such affidavit shall not be made by the candidate. Each and every candidate shall make and file his affidavit stating that he is eligible to the office for the township, county, district or state in which he is and will be a bona fide candidate for nomination for said office, and shall file such affidavit with the said nomination paper or papers, when such paper or papers are required. If no such paper or papers are required, then he shall file such affidavit alone, or there shall be filed a nomination paper signed by ten qualified voters of any subdivision of a county, with the county auditor, at least fifteen days prior to such primary election, and the filing of such affidavit or such nomination paper shall entitle such candidate to have his name printed on the official primary ballot of his party. Such affidavit shall be in form and substance as follows:

"I, ...being duly sworn, say that I reside at...................................street, (city or town) of...................................... county of...in the state of Iowa; that I am eligible to the office for which I am a candidate, and that the political party with which I affiliate is the...party; that I am a candidate for nomination to the office of.. to be made at the primary election to be held in June, 19........, and hereby request that my name be printed upon the official primary ballot as provided by law, as a candidate of the...party. I furthermore declare that if I am nominated and elected I will qualify as such officer.

(Signed)..

Subscribed and sworn to (or affirmed) before me.. by.....................................on this.....................day of...................................., 19.........

....;"

The nomination papers above required shall be signed as follows:

(1). If for a state office, United States senator, or elector at large, by at least one per centum of the voters of the party (as shown by the returns of the last general election) of such candidates, in each of at least ten counties of the state, and in the aggregate not less than one-half of one per centum of the total vote of his party in the state, as shown by the last general election.

(2). If for a representative in congress, district elector, or senator in the general assembly in districts composed of more than one county, by at least two per centum of the voters of his party, as shown by the last general election, in at least one-half of the counties of the district, and in the aggregate not less than one per centum of the total vote of his party in such district, as shown by the last general election.

(3). If for an office to be filled by the voters of the county, by at least two per centum of the party vote in the county, as shown by the last general election.

In each of the above cases, the vote to be taken for the purpose of computing the percentage shall be the vote cast for the head of the ticket. All nomination papers shall be destroyed at the same time and in the manner in which the primary election ballots are destroyed.* [35 G. A., ch. 110, § 1; 33 G. A., ch. 69, § 4; 32 G. A., ch. 51, § 10.]

Sec. 1087-a12. **Nomination certified to county auditor— order on ballot designated—notice published.** At least thirty days before any such primary election, the secretary of state shall transmit to each county auditor a certified list containing the name and postoffice address of each person for whom a nomination paper has been filed in his office, in accordance with the provisions of section ten[1] of this act and entitled to be voted for at such primary election by the voters of such county, together with a designation of the office for which he is a candidate, and the party from which he seeks a nomination.

Such lists shall also designate the order in which the names of all candidates for the office of senator in the congress of the United States and for offices to be filled by the voters of the entire state shall be arranged and printed upon the primary election ballots in each county, in the following manner, to wit: The secretary of state shall prepare a list of the counties of the state for each political party by arranging the various counties in the order of the vote cast by each political party in each county for its candidate for governor at the last preceding general election, or for the head of the ticket of any political party when it had no candidate for governor at such election, numbering the counties consecutively on each list from one to

---

*Remaining portion of Sec. 1087-a10, supplement to the code, 1913, is rendered inoperative by amendment to the U. S. constitution (Art. XVII) and by Sec. 1087-c.

[1]Sec. 1087-a10.

3

ninety-nine, both inclusive, beginning with the county which cast the largest vote, which shall be numbered "1." He shall then arrange the surnames of such candidates in alphabetical order for the respective offices for the several political parties for the first county on the respective lists; thereafter, for each succeeding county, the names appearing first for the respective offices in the last preceding county shall be placed last, so that the names that occupied second position before the change shall occupy first position after the change. Such auditor shall forthwith publish a proclamation of the time of holding the primary election, the hours during which the polls will be open, the offices for which candidates are to be nominated and that the primary election will be held in the regular polling places in each precinct. Such notice shall be published once each week for two consecutive weeks before the primary election, in not to exceed two newspapers of general circulation in such county. One of such newspapers shall represent the political party which cast the largest vote in such county at the last preceding general election, and the other, if any, that shall represent the political party which cast the next largest vote in such county at such general election. The county auditor shall correct any errors or omissions in the names of candidates and any other errors brought to his knowledge before the printing of the ballots. [33 G. A., ch. 69, § 5; 32 G. A., ch. 51, § 12.]

Sec. 1087-a14. Ballot—form. The official primary election ballot shall be prepared, arranged and printed substantially in the following form:

.

..............................PRIMARY ELECTION BALLOT

(Name of Party)

of

...............................Township or Precinct, ...Ward,

City or town of.........................., County of...................., State of Iowa.

Primary election held on the...day of June, 19.........

For United States Senator.

(Vote for one.)

☐ William K. Brown

☐ J. R. Wayne

☐ ....

For Governor.

(Vote for one.)

☐ Howard Collins

☐ William Longley

☐ ....

(Followed by other elective state and district officers in order.)

For County Auditor.

(Vote for one.)

☐ William Strong

☐ Robert Thompson

☐ ....

(Followed by other elective county officers in order.)

For Delegates to County Convention.

(Vote for................)

☐ ....

☐ ....

☐ ....

☐ ....

☐ ....

For Township Clerk.

(Vote for one.)

☐ John H. Black

☐ Joseph Raymond

☐ ....

For Township Trustees.

(Vote for two.)

☐ Clarence Foster

☐ William Jones

☐ H. S. Wilson

☐ ....

(Followed by other elective township officers in order.)

For Party Committeeman.

(Vote for one.)

☐ John Doe

☐ Richard Roe

☐ ....

[33 G. A., ch. 69, § 7; 32 G. A., ch. 51, § 14.]

Sec. 1087-a13. **Printing—order of names on ballot.** The names of the candidates of each political party for nomination for the several offices, and for party committeemen and blank spaces for the delegates to the county convention shall be printed in black ink on separate sheets of paper, uniform in color, quality, texture and size, with the name of the political party printed at the head of said ballots, which ballots shall be prepared by the county auditor in the same manner as for the general election, except as in this chapter otherwise provided. The names of candidates for the office of senator in the congress of the United States and for offices to be filled by the voters of the entire state shall be arranged and printed on the primary election ballots in the order in which they are certified by the secretary of state. The names of candidates for offices to be filled by the voters of a county, and by the voters of any district of the state composed of more than one county, shall be arranged and printed upon the primary election ballots in the following manner, to wit: The county auditor shall prepare a list of the election precincts of his county, by arranging the various townships, towns and cities in the county in alphabetical order and the wards or precincts of each city, town or township in numerical order under the name of such city, town or township. He shall then arrange the surnames of all candidates for such offices alphabetically for the respective offices for the first precinct in the list; thereafter, for each succeeding precinct, the names appearing first for the respective offices in the last preceding precinct shall be placed last, so that the names that were second before the change shall be first after the change. The names of candidates for all offices to be filled by the voters of a territory smaller than a county shall be arranged and printed alphabetically according to surnames for the respective offices. [33 G. A., ch. 69, § 6; 32 G. A., ch. 51, § 13.]

Sec. 1087-a15. Sample ballots. After the printing of the official ballots, the county auditor shall change a sufficient number thereof to supply each voting precinct in the county with ten sample ballots of each political party. The auditor shall change the same by writing or stamping the words "sample ballot" in red ink near the top of such ballots, and by signing his name or stamping a facsimile thereof and his title of office immediately thereunder. Such sample ballots shall not be voted, received or counted in any primary election. The county auditor shall distribute such sample ballots with the official ballots, and it shall be the duty of the judges of election to see that such sample ballots are posted in and about the polling places upon the day of the primary election and before the opening of the polls. [33 G. A., ch. 69, § 8; 32 G. A., ch. 51, § 15.]

Sec. 1087-a5. Judges and clerks—how selected—oath—expenses. The judges and clerks of all primary elections under this act shall be made up and selected and appointed in the same manner as for the general election held in November, and they shall take the same oath and the judges are hereby authorized to administer oaths as hereinafter provided. Vacancies shall be filled as provided for the judges and clerks of the general election. The expenses of the primary election shall be audited by the board of supervisors of each county and be paid the same as the expenses of the general election. The compensation of the judges and clerks of the primary election shall be the sum of thirty cents per hour for all official services rendered by any such judge or clerk at any such election. [36 G. A., ch. 215, § 1; 33 G. A., ch. 69, § 2; 32 G. A., ch. 51, § 5.]

Sec. 1087-a16. Supplies—poll books. All necessary election supplies, including poll books as provided by law, for the general election, together with a sufficient number of official primary ballots of each party, shall be furnished for the primary election board for each precinct by the county auditor, and such poll books shall contain blank spaces for the names of the candidates of the several parties for the different offices to be written in, and blank spaces for entering by the clerks the names of the electors voting at said primary election; and upon the pages provided for entering the names of said voters there shall be ruled spaces for the listing of the names of said voters and for the designation of the party ticket voted by said elector in manner and form substantially as follows:

No.	Name	Republican	Democrat	Prohibition	Socialist
1	James Smith	X			
2	Tom Jones		X		
3	Dan Brown			X	
4	George White				X

It shall be the duty of the clerks of the primary election when entering the name of a voter to place in the poll books a cross, thus (X), in the column designating the party ticket which was given to said voter upon his application for a ticket. [32 G. A., ch. 51, § 16.]

Sec. 1087-a6. **Australian ballot—polls open—ballots.** The Australian ballot system as now used in this state, except as hereinafter provided, shall be used at said primary election in all precincts. The voter shall in all cases mark the ballot in the square before the name of each person for whom he desires to vote. In cities where registration is required by law, the polls shall be open from seven [o'clock] a. m. to eight [o'clock] p. m., and in all other precincts from nine o'clock a. m. to eight o'clock p. m. The elector voting at said primary election shall be allowed to vote for candidates for nomination on the ticket of only one political party, and that shall be the party with which he is registered as affiliated. The endorsement of the judges of election and the facsimile of the auditor's signature shall appear upon the ballots as provided by law for the ballots used for the November election. The voter shall return the ballot, folded, to one of the judges of election who shall deposit it in the ballot box. If any primary elector write upon his ticket the name of any person who is a candidate for the same office upon some other party ticket than that upon which his name shall be so written, such ballot shall be so counted for such person only as a candidate of the party upon whose ballot his name is written, and shall in no case be counted for such person as a candidate upon any other ticket. In case the person is nominated upon more than one ticket, he shall forthwith file with the proper officer a written declaration indicating the party designation under which his name is to be printed on the official ballot for the general election following such primary election. [33 G. A., ch. 69, § 3; 32 G. A., ch. 51, § 6.]

Sec. 1087-a7. **First declaration of party affiliation—record.** At the primary election to be held in June in the year nineteen hundred eight any person shall be entitled to participate therein who is a qualified elector in such precinct at the time of said primary election, and when the voter seeks to pass the guard rail he shall indicate the party ballot he desires, and one of the judges of the primary election board shall give him such primary ballot (unless challenged, and if so challenged, then only in the event that the challenge is determined in favor of the voter), and such person shall thereupon be allowed to vote. The voter's selection shall constitute his declaration of party affiliation, and it shall be the duty of the primary election board to record his name and check his declaration of party affiliation on the poll books used by the clerks of the primary election board, and said list properly certified to by said primary election board shall be returned to the county auditor for preservation. Copies of the names and party entries on such list, together with the changes of party affiliation as hereinafter provided, arranged alphabetically by surnames, shall be used at subsequent primaries for determining with what party the voter has been enrolled, and no voter enrolled under the provisions of this act shall be allowed to receive the ballot of any political party except that with which he is enrolled, but he may change his enrollment as hereinafter provided. The county auditor shall prepare for each voting precinct two ·of the above mentioned lists duly certified by him, and taken from the poll books of the last preceding primary election, which he shall deliver to the succeeding primary election boards in the year nineteen hundred ten and biennially thereafter, at least one day prior to the day of the primary election, and which lists together with the poll books of the primary election shall be returned to the said auditor in good condition within twenty-four hours after the primary election, to be preserved by him. [32 G. A., ch. 51, § 7.]

Sec. 1087-a8. Change of affiliation—first voter—removal. Any person who has thus declared his party affiliation shall thereafter be listed on the poll books as a member of that political party, and such person while a resident of the same voting precinct need not declare his party affiliation at succeeding primary elections unless he desires to change his party affiliation. Any elector, who, having declared his party affiliation, desires to change the same, may, not less than ten days prior to the date of any primary election, file a written declaration with the county auditor stating his change of party affiliation, and the auditor shall enter a record of such change on the poll books of the last preceding primary election in the proper column opposite the voter's name and on the voting list. Any elector whose party affiliation has for any reason not been registered or any elector who has changed his residence to another precinct, or a first voter or citizen of this state casting his first vote in this state shall be entitled to vote at any subsequent primary election in the same manner and upon the same terms as provided in section seven of this act, and the clerks of the primary election shall record his party affiliation and the county auditor shall add his name to the alphabetical lists for use in subsequent primary elections as provided for in section seven of this act. [32 G. A., ch. 51, § 8.]

Sec. 1087-a9. **Challengers—affidavit.** Each political party shall be entitled to have two party challengers present at each polling place, to be appointed by the respective party committeemen. Any judge or clerk of the primary election or any party challenger may challenge any voter upon the grounds mentioned in section eleven hundred fifteen of the code and such challenge shall be determined as there provided. Any elector whose party affiliation has been recorded as provided by this act and who desires to change his party affiliation on the primary election day, shall be subject to challenge. If the person challenged insists that he is entitled to vote the ticket of the political party to which he has transferred his political affiliation and the challenge is not withdrawn, one of the judges shall tender to him the following oath: "You do solemnly swear (or affirm) that you have in good faith changed your party affiliation to and desire to be a member of the .... party." And if he take such oath he shall thereupon be given a ticket of such political party and the clerks of the primary election shall change his enrollment of party affiliation accordingly. [32 G. A., ch. 51, § 9.]

Sec. 1087-a17. **Ballots counted—returns.** Upon the closing of the polls the clerks and judges shall immediately open the ballot box and proceed to take therefrom the ballots. Said officers shall count the number of ballots cast for each party, at the same time bunching the tickets cast for each party, in separate piles. As soon as the clerks and judges shall have sorted the ballots of each party, separately, they shall take the tally sheets provided in the poll books and shall count all the ballots for each party separately until the count is completed, and shall certify to the number of votes cast for each candidate for each office upon the ticket of each party. After all have been counted and certified to by the clerk and judges, they shall seal the ballots cast by each of the parties in separate envelopes, on the outside of which shall be printed or written the names of that party's candidates for the different offices, and opposite each candidate's name shall be placed the number of votes cast for such candidate in said precinct, and then seal the envelopes containing the votes of the different political parties, in one large envelope, on the outside of which, or on a paper attached thereto, shall be printed or written, in perpendicular columns, the names of the several political parties with the names of the candidates for the different offices under their respective party headings, and opposite each candidate's name shall be placed the number of votes cast for such candidate in said precinct, and at the bottom the total vote cast by each political party in said precinct, and such envelopes shall be returned to the county auditor, who shall carefully preserve the same in said condition and deliver them to the county board of canvassers. But any elector of the county shall have the right, before the day fixed for canvassing the returns, to ascertain the vote cast for any candidate in any precinct in the county, as shown on the outside of the large envelope. Said judges of election shall deliver the returns so made, together .with the poll books, including tally sheets and certificates of the judges and clerks written thereon, to the county auditor within twenty-four hours after the primary election has closed; and if the returns from any precinct be not so delivered within the said time, the county auditor shall forthwith send a messenger for any such missing returns, and said messenger shall be paid, as provided by law, for the general election. [32 G. A., ch. 51, § 17.]

Sec. 1087-a19—Canvass by board of supervisors—certificates. On the second Tuesday next following the primary election in June, the board of supervisors shall meet, open, and canvass the returns from each voting precinct in the county, and make abstracts thereof, stating in words written at length the number of ballots cast in the county by each political party, separately, for each office, the name of each person voted for and the number of votes given to each person for each different office and shall sign and certify thereto and file the same with the county auditor. Such canvass and certificate shall be final as to all candidates for nomination to any elective county office or office of a subdivision of a county; and the candidate or candidates of each political party for each office to be filled by the voters of any subdivision of a county having received the highest number of votes shall be duly and legally nominated as the candidate of his party for such office. Provided, however, that no candidate whose name is not printed on the official primary ballot, who receives less than five per centum of the votes cast in such subdivision for governor on the party ticket with which he affiliates, at the last general election, nor less than five votes shall be declared to have been nominated to any such office; and the candidate or candidates of each political party for each office to be filled by the voters of the county having received the highest number of votes, and not less than thirty-five per centum of all the votes cast by the party for such office, shall be duly and legally nominated as the candidate of his party for such office. Provided, however, that no candidate whose name is not printed on the official ballot who receives less than ten per centum of the whole number of votes cast in the county for governor on the party ticket with which he affiliates, at the last general election shall be declared to have been nominated to any such office; and each candidate so nominated shall be entitled to have his name printed on the official ballot to be voted for at the general election without other certificate, and the board shall prepare and certify a list of the candidates of each party so nominated, separately, and deliver to the chairman of each party central committee for the county a copy of the list of candidates nominated by the party he represents; and shall also prepare, certify and deliver to such chairman a list of the offices to be filled by the voters of a county for which no candidate of his party was nominated, together with the names of the candidate for each of such offices voted for at the primary election and the number of votes received by each of such candidates. [34 G. A., ch. 59, § 1; 34 G. A., ch. 58, § 2; 33 G. A., ch. 69, § 10; 32 G. A., ch. 51, § 19.]

Sec. 1087-a18. **Recount of ballots.** Any candidate whose name appears upon the official primary ballot of any voting precinct may require the board of supervisors of the county in which such precinct is situated to recount the ballots cast in any such precinct as to the office for which he was a candidate, at the time fixed for canvassing the returns of the judges of election, by filing with the county auditor not later than the day before such meeting, a showing in writing, duly sworn to by such candidate, that fraud was committed, or error or mistake made, in counting or returning the votes cast in any such precinct as to the office for which he was a candidate. The showing must be specified and from it there must appear reasonable ground to believe that a recount of the ballots would produce a result as to his candidacy different from the returns made by the judges. If such showing is made to the satisfaction of the board, it shall thereupon recount the ballots cast in any such precinct for the office for which the contestant was a candidate, and if the result reached by the board on the recount of the ballots as to such office be different from that returned by the judges of election it shall be substituted therefor as the true and correct return and so regarded in all subsequent proceedings. The action of the board shall be final and no other contest of any kind shall be permitted. The term "candidate" as used in this section shall include and apply to persons voted for for delegates and party committeemen. [33 G. A., ch. 69, § 9; 32 G. A., ch. 51, § 18.]

Sec. 1087-a20. Abstracts forwarded to secretary of state. The county board of canvassers shall also make a separate abstract of the canvass as to the following offices and certify to the same and forthwith forward it to the secretary of state, viz.:

United States senator,

Electors of the president and vice president of the United States,

All state offices,

Representative in congress,

Senators and representatives in the general assembly. [32 G. A., ch. 51, § 20.]

Sec. 1087-a21. County returns filed—published proceedings of canvassing board. When the canvass is concluded, the board shall deliver the original returns to the auditor, who shall file the same and record each of the abstracts above mentioned in the. election book. The published proceedings of the board of supervisors as a canvassing board shall contain only a brief statement of the names of the candidates nominated by the electors of any county or subdivision thereof under the title of the office for which they are nominated, and a statement of the title of the office for which they are nominated, and a statement of the title of the county offices, if any, for which no nomination was made by any political party participating in the primary election for the failure of any one of its candidates for any office to receive thirty-five per centum of all the votes cast by the party for such office. [36 G. A., ch. 102, § 1; 33 G. A., ch. 69, § 11; 32 G. A., ch. 51, § 21.]

Sec. 1087-a22. Canvass by state board—certificates. On the second Monday after the June primary election, the executive council shall meet as a canvassing board, and open and canvass the abstract returns received from each county in the state. If returns are not received from all the counties, the secretary of state shall immediately send a messenger after the abstract returns and the board may adjourn from day to day until they are received. The board shall make an abstract of its canvass, stating in words written at length, the number of ballots cast by each political party, separately, for each office designated in section twenty hereof, the names of all the persons voted for, and the number of votes received by each person for each office, and shall sign and certify thereto. Such canvass and certificates shall be final as to all candidates named therein; and the candidate of each political party for each office to be filled by vote of the people, including the office of senator in the congress of the United States, having received the highest number of votes in the state or district of the state, as the case may be, provided he received not less than thirty-five per centum of all the votes cast by the party for such office, shall be duly and legally nominated as the candidate of his party for such office, provided however that no candidate whose name is not printed on the official ballot who receives less than ten per centum of the whole number of votes cast in the state or district of the state as the case may be, for governor on the party ticket with which he affiliates, at the last general election shall be declared to have been nominated to any such office and each candidate so nominated shall be entitled to have his name printed on the official ballot to be voted at the general election without other certificate; and the board shall prepare and certify a list of the candidates of each party so nominated, separately, and deliver to the chairman of each party central committee for the state a copy of the list of candidates nominated by the party he represents; and shall also forthwith prepare a certificate as to each office, separately, for which no candidate was nominated, by reason of the failure of any candidate for any such office to receive thirty-five per centum of all votes cast by such party for such office, together with the names of the several candidates for each of such offices voted for at the primary election and the number of votes received by each of such candidates and send such certificate to the chairman of the party central committee for the state, in case of offices to be filled by the voters of the entire state, and to the chairman of the party central committee for a district of the state, if known, in case of offices to be filled by the voters of any such district of the state composed of more than one county, and to the county auditor of each county in any such district, and to the county auditor and the chairman of the party central committee for the county, in case any such district is composed of one county. The candidate of any party for the office of senator in the congress of the United States having received the highest number of votes of his party in the state, shall be the nominee of his party for such office.* (38 G. A., ch. 253; 35 G. A., ch. 109, § 2; 33 G. A., ch. 69, § 12; 32 G. A., ch. 51, § 22.]

Sec. 1087-a23. **State returns filed—nominations certified to county auditor.** When the canvass is concluded, the board shall deliver the original abstract returns to the secretary of state, who shall file the same in his office and record the abstracts of the canvass of the state board and certificates attached thereto in the book kept by him known as the election book; and not less than fifteen days before the general election he shall certify to the auditor of each county, under separate party headings, the name of each person nominated as shown by the official canvass made by the executive council, or as certified to him by the proper persons when any person has been nominated by a convention or party committee, his place of residence, the office to which he is nominated, and the order in which the tickets of the several political parties shall appear on the official ballot. Should a vacancy in the nominations occur and be filled after such certificate has been forwarded, a like certificate shall at once be made and sent to the proper officer together with a statement showing the reason for its subsequent issue. [33 G. A., ch. 69, § 17; 32 G. A., ch. 51, § 23.]

Sec. 1087-a24. **Tie vote—vacancies.** In case of a tie vote resulting in no nomination for any office, or election of delegates or party committeeman, the tie shall forthwith be determined by lot by the board of canvassers, or judges of election,

---

*Remaining portion of this section is now obsolete.

as the case may be. Vacancies occurring in nominations made in the primary election before the holding of the county, district or state convention, shall be filled by the county convention if the office in which the vacancy in nomination occurs is to be filled by the voters of the county; by a district convention if the office in which the vacancy in nomination occurs is to be filled by the voters of a district composed of more than one county; by the state convention if the office in which the vacancy occurs is to be filled by the voters of the entire state. Vacancies in nominations in such offices occurring after the holding of a county, district or state convention, or on failure of any such convention to fill a vacancy in a nomination, as aforesaid, then it shall be filled by the party committee for the county, district or state, as the case may be. If a vacancy shall occur in any such office too late for the filing of nomination papers for candidates therefor in the primary election and before the holding of a county, district or state convention, as the case may be, then the convention having jurisdiction shall make nomination for such office; and if a vacancy in any such office shall occur after the holding of a county, district or state convention, then nomination for such office may be made by the party committee for the county, district or state, as the case may be. Vacancies in nominations for offices to be filled by the voters of a territory smaller than a county shall be filled by the members of the party committee for the county from such subdivision. Nominations made as above provided and as provided in sections ten hundred eighty-seven-a twenty-five, ten hundred eighty-seven-a twenty-six and ten hundred eighty-seven-a twenty-seven of the supplement to the code, 1907, shall be certified forthwith to the proper officer by the chairman and secretary of the convention or committee as the case may be, and if received in time shall be printed upon the official ballots the same as if the nomination had been made in the primary election. Such certificate of nomination shall state the name, place of residence, and postoffice address of the person nominated, the office to which he is nominated and the name of the political party making the nomination. [35 G. A., ch. 109, § 9; 33 G. A., ch. 69, § 13; 32 Ex. G. A., ch. 1, § 1; 32 G. A., ch. 51, § 24.]

Sec. 1087-a24a. **United States senator—vacancy—nomination.** In case of death, withdrawal, or inability to act, for any cause, of a party's candidate for senator in the congress of the United States, as expressed in the regular June primary, such vacancy shall be filled by the state convention of said party, held in accordance with the provisions of section ten hundred eighty-seven-a twenty-seven of the supplement to the code, 1907; provided that if such vacancy occurs after the holding of said convention and thirty days prior to the holding of the regular November election, said delegates to said convention shall be reconvened within ten days after such vacancy has occurred, by the chairman of said party's state central committee, and a party candidate shall be named in said convention to fill such vacancy.* [35 G. A., ch. 109, § 9; 32 Ex. G. A., ch. 1, § 1.]

Sec. 1087-a25. County convention—delegates—committeemen. In each county there shall be held in each year in which a general election in November is to take place a county convention of each political party. Said county convention shall be composed of delegates elected at the last preceding primary election, and shall be held on the fourth Saturday following the primary election, convening at eleven o'clock a. m. The number of delegates from each voting precinct shall be determined by a ratio adopted by the respective party county central committees, and shall be thus determined and a statement designating the number from each voting precinct in the county filed in the office of the county auditor at least thirty days before the primary election; if not so done, the auditor shall fix the number. The requisite number of names of candidates of his choice for delegates to the county convention to which each precinct is entitled shall be written, or pasted with uniform white pasters, on the blank lines upon the ballot by the voter while in the booth, or by someone designated by a voter unable to write, after the ballots are received and before they are deposited, and the requisite number of persons from each precinct who receive the highest number of votes shall be the delegates from the precinct to the county convention. The term of office of such delegate shall begin on the day following the final canvass of the votes by the board of supervisors, and shall continue for two years and until their successors are elected. One member of the county central committee for each political party from each precinct shall be elected. His term

---

*Remaining portion of Sec. 1087-a24a, supplement to the code. 1913, is rendered inoperative by amendment to the U. S. constitution (Art. XVII) and by Sec. 1087-c.

of office shall begin on the day of the county convention and immediately following the adjournment thereof and shall continue for two years and until his successor is elected and qualified, unless such committeeman shall be removed by the county central committee for inattention to the duties of his position, incompetency or failure to support the ticket nominated by the party which elected him to such position. The county central committee elected in the primary election shall organize on the day of the convention, immediately following the same. Vacancies in such committee may be filled by majority vote of the committee. Returns shall be made by the judges of election respecting delegates and members of the county central committee in the same manner as for other offices, except that the judges of election shall canvass the returns as to delegates and members of the county central committee, and certify the result to the auditor with the returns. The auditor shall, immediately after the final count and canvass of the votes and returns by the board of supervisors, notify the delegates and members of the county central committee who have thus been elected, of their election, and of the time and place of holding the county convention, and shall on the second Thursday following the primary election, deliver a certified list thereof to the chairmen of the respective party central committees for the county. When the delegates, or a majority thereof, or when delegates representing a majority of the precincts, thus elected, shall have assembled in the county convention at the time herein prescribed and at the county seat, the convention shall be called to order by the chairman of the county central committee, who shall present the certified list of delegates and members of the county central committee, and a list of the offices for which no nomination was made at the primary election, by reason of the failure of any candidate for any such office to receive thirty-five per centum of all votes cast by such party therefor. If any precinct shall not be fully represented the delegates present from such precinct shall cast the full vote thereof, but there shall be no proxies. The said county convention shall make nominations of candidates for the party for any office to be filled by the voters of a county when no candidate for such office has been nominated at the preceding primary election by reason of the failure of any candidate for any such office to receive thirty-five per centum of all votes cast by such party therefor, as shown by the canvass of the returns provided for in section nineteen[1] of this act, and shall nominate candidates for the office of judge of the district court in counties comprising one judicial district of the state,[2] and shall select delegates to the next ensuing state and district conventions of that year upon such ratio of representation as may be determined by the party organization for the state, district or districts of the state, as the case may be, but no delegates shall be so selected to any of the district conventions referred to in section twenty-six[3] of this act, except judicial conventions, unless a call therefor has been issued as therein provided.   The said county convention shall also elect a member of the party central committee for the senatorial, judicial, and congressional districts composed of more than one county.   But in no case shall the county convention make a nomination for an office for which no person was voted for in the primary election of such party, except for judges of the superior and district courts. [33 G. A., ch. 69, § 14; 32 G. A., ch. 51, § 25.]

Sec. 1087-a26.   District convention.   In any senatorial, judicial, or congressional district composed of more than one county, in any year in which a senator in the general assembly, a judge of the district court, or a representative in the congress of the United States, is to be elected, a senatorial or congressional convention may be held, and a judicial convention shall be held by each political party participating in the primary election of that year.   Not less than ten days and not more than sixty days before the day fixed for holding the county convention a call for such senatorial, judicial and congressional convention to be held shall be issued by the party central committee for any such district and published in at least one newspaper of general circulation of each county composing any such district and which call shall state among other things the number of delegates each county of the district shall be entitled to and the time and place of holding the convention.   Any such call shall be signed by the chairman of the party central committee for any such district, and be filed by him with the county auditor not less than five days before the county convention and the county auditor shall attach a true copy thereof to the certified list of delegates required to be

[1]See Sec. 1087-a19.
[2]See Sec. 1087-b2.
[3]See Sec. 1087-a26.

4

delivered by him to the chairmen of the respective party county central committees. In case no nomination was made in the primary election for the office of senator in the general assembly in any district composed of more than one county, or for the office of representative in congress of the United States, by reason of the failure of any candidate for any office to receive thirty-five per centum of all votes cast by his party therefor, as shown by the certificate issued by the state board of canvassers provided for in this act, then in any such district the chairman of the party central committee therefor shall forthwith issue such call for a convention in such district and deliver the same to the county auditor of each county in the district and in such case said call need not be published. No such district convention shall be held earlier than the first Thursday or later than the fifth Thursday following the county convention. The convention when organized shall make nominations of candidates for the party for any such district office when no candidate for such office has been nominated at the preceding primary election, by reason of the failure of any candidate for any such office to receive thirty-five per centum of all votes cast by such party therefor, as shown by the canvass of the votes provided for in section twenty-two[1] hereof. The organization of and procedure in any such district convention shall be the same as in the state convention. Such district conventions may adopt party platforms and transact such other business as may properly be brought before them. But in no case shall any such convention of a party make a nomination for an office for which no person was voted for in the primary election of such party, except for judges of the district court. [33 G. A., ch. 69, § 15; 32 G. A., ch. 51, § 26.]

Sec. 1087-a27. **State convention—state central committee.** A state convention of each political party, composed of delegates chosen in the manner herein provided, shall be held not earlier than the first Wednesday and not later than the fifth Wednesday following the county convention, in the year nineteen hundred and eight, and biennially thereafter, convening at such time and place as may be determined upon by the party organization. The convention shall be called to order by the chairman of the state central committee, who shall thereupon present a list of delegates, as certified by the various county

[1]See Sec. 1087-a22.

conventions, and effect a temporary organization. If any county shall not be fully represented, the delegates present from such county shall cast the full vote thereof, but there shall be no proxies. Such convention when permanently organized shall formulate and adopt the state platform of the party it represents, and shall make nominations of candidates for the party for any state office to be filled by the voters of the entire state, including the office of senator in the congress of the United States, when no candidate for such office has been nominated at the preceding primary election, by reason of the failure of any candidate for any such office to receive thirty-five per centum of all votes cast by such party therefor, as shown by the canvass of the returns provided for in section twenty-two[1] hereof; and shall nominate candidates for the office of judge of the supreme court. It shall also elect a state central committee consisting of not less than one member from each congressional district and transact such other business as may properly be brought before it. The state central committee elected at said state convention may organize at pleasure for political work as is usual and customary with such committees and shall continue to act until succeeded by another committee duly elected. But in no case shall the state convention of a party make a nomination for an office for which no person was voted for in the primary election of such party, except for judges of the supreme court. [35 G. A., ch. 109, § 3; 33 G. A., ch. 69, § 16; 32 G. A., ch. 51, § 27.]

Sec. 1087-a28. **Existing party committees.** The regularly organized political committees of each party as at present or hereafter constituted may continue to act until supplanted by the committees elected under the provisions of this act. [32 G. A., ch. 51, § 28.]

Sec. 1087-a34. **Primary elections in certain cities.** The provisions of this act shall, so far as applicable, govern the nominations of candidates by political parties for all offices to be filled by a direct vote of the people in cities of the first class and cities acting under a special charter having a population of over fifteen thousand, except all such special charter cities and cities of the first class as have by vote of the people adopted a plan of municipal government which specifically provides for a nonpartisan primary election. The duties de-

[1]See Sec. 1087-a22.

volving upon the county auditor, by the foregoing provisions of this act, shall, in municipal elections, devolve upon the city auditor and the duties devolving upon the board of supervisors by the foregoing provisions of this act [shall] devolve upon the city council which shall meet to perform said duties within two days next following the primary election. The date of the municipal primary election shall be the last Monday in February of each year in which a municipal election is held in said cities, after the year nineteen hundred seven, and the percentage of voters signing petitions required for printing the name of a candidate upon the official primary ballot shall be the same as is required of a candidate for a county office and shall be based upon the vote cast for mayor by the respective parties in the preceding city election. The names of candidates for ward aldermen, for city precinct committeemen and for delegates to the city convention, shall not be printed upon the official primary ballot but in each case a blank line or lines shall be provided therefor. A plurality shall nominate the party candidate for alderman and a plurality shall elect the precinct committeemen and delegates to the city convention. The entire expense of conducting a primary election provided for in this section shall be audited by the city council and paid by the city. This section shall not be held to repeal any law which provides for the adoption of a plan of municipal government by vote of the people and which embraces a nonpartisan primary election. [32 G. A., ch. 51, § 35.]

Sec. 1087-a35. **Repeal.** Chapter forty of the laws of the thirtieth general assembly, relating to primary elections; and chapters forty-five and forty-six of the laws of the thirty-first general assembly, relating to primary elections, are hereby repealed. [32 G. A., ch. 51, § 34.]

Sec. 1087-a31. **Misconduct of election officials—penalty.** Any party committeeman or any primary election or other public officer upon whom a duty is imposed by this act or by acts herein made applicable to primary elections, who shall wilfully neglect to perform any such duty, or who shall wilfully perform it in such a way as to hinder the objects thereof, or shall disclose to anyone, except as may be ordered by any court of justice, the contents of any ballot or any part thereof, as to the manner in which the same may have been voted, shall be punished by a fine of not less than one hundred dollars nor more than one thousand dollars, or by imprisoment in the penitentiary not to exceed five years, or by both such fine and imprisonment. [32 G. A., ch. 51, § 31.]

Sec. 1087-a29. **Nomination by petition.** Nothing contained in this act shall be construed so as to prohibit nomination of candidates for office by petition as now authorized by law; but no person so nominated shall be permitted to use the name of any political party authorized or entitled under this act to nominate a ticket by primary vote or that has nominated a ticket by primary vote under the provisions of this act. [32 G. A., ch. 51, § 29.]

Sec. 1087-a30. **Special elections.** This act shall not apply to special elections to fill vacancies. [32 G. A., ch. 51, § 30.]

DIVISION VIII.
NOMINATION BY CONVENTION, OR PETITION.

Sec. 1098. **Nomination by convention.** Any convention of delegates, and any primary, caucus or meeting of qualified electors, representing a political party which, at the general election next preceding, polled at least two per cent of the entire vote cast in the state, may, for the state, or any division or municipality thereof for which the same is held, make one nomination of a candidate for each office therein to be filled at the election, and any such convention, primary, caucus or meeting, representing a political party which, at the general election next preceding, polled at least two per cent of the entire vote cast in any division or municipality of the state, may, for such division or municipality, or for any political subdivision thereof for which the same is held, make one such nomination for each office therein to be filled at the election. [24 G. A., ch. 33, § 4.]

Sec. 1099. **Certificates.** Certificates of nominations, made as provided in the preceding section, shall, besides containing the names of candidates, specify as to each:

1. The office to which he is nominated;

2. The party making such nomination, or political principle which he represents, expressed in not more than five words;

3. His place of residence, with the street and number thereof, if any.

In case of electors for president and vice president of the United States, the names of the candidates for president and vice president shall be added to the party or political name. Every such certificate of nomination shall be signed by the presiding officer and secretary of the convention, caucus or meeting of qualified electors, or by the board of canvassers to which the returns of such primary election are made, each of whom shall add to his signature his place of residence, and shall be sworn to by each signer thereof to be true to the best of his knowledge and belief, and a certificate of the oath shall be annexed to the certificate of nomination. The presiding officer and secretary of each convention, primary, caucus or meeting shall also certify, to the officer with whom the nomination certificates are filed, the names and addresses of each of the members of the executive or central committee appointed or elected by or representing it, and the provisions, if any, made by it for filling vacancies in nominations; and this may be done in the nomination certificate, or by a separate certificate. [38 G. A., ch. 86, § 1; 24 G. A., ch. 33, §§ 4, 6.]

Sec. 1103. Objections. All objections or other questions arising in relation to certificates of nomination or nomination papers shall be filed with the officer with whom the certificate of nomination or nomination papers to which objection is made are filed. Those with the secretary of state shall be filed not less than twenty days, and those with other officers not less than eight days, before the day of election, except that nominations to fill vacancies occurring after said time, or in case of nomination made to be voted on at a special election, objections shall be filed within three days after the filing of the certificate or nomination papers. Objections filed with the secretary of state shall be considered by the secretary and auditor of state and attorney general, and a majority decision shall be final; but if the objection is to the certificate or nomination papers of one or more of the above named officers, said officer or officers so objected to shall not pass upon the same, but their places shall be filled, respectively, by the treasurer of state, the governor, and the superintendent of public instruction. Objections filed with the county auditor shall be considered by the county auditor, clerk of the district court and county attorney, and a majority decision shall be final; but if the objection is to the certificate or nomination papers of one or more of the above named county officers, said officer or officers so objected to shall not pass upon such objection, but their places shall be filled, respectively, by the county treasurer, the sheriff and county superintendent. Objections filed with the city or town clerk shall be considered by the mayor and clerk and one member of the council chosen by the council by ballot, and a majority decision shall be final; but if the objection is to the certificate or nomination papers of either of said city or town officials, he shall not pass upon said objection, but his place shall be filled by a member of the council against whom no such objection exists, chosen as above provided. When any of the above objections are made, notice shall forthwith be given to the candidate affected thereby, addressed to his place of residence as given in the certificate or nomination papers, stating that objections have been made to his certificate or nomination papers, also stating the time and place such objections will be considered. [24 G. A., ch. 33, § 10.]

Sec. 1100. Nominations by petition. Nominations for candidates for state offices may also be made by nomination paper or papers signed by not less than five hundred qualified voters of the state; for county, district or other division, not less than a county, by such paper or papers signed by not less than twenty-five qualified voters, residents of such county, district or division; and for township, city, town or ward, by such paper or papers signed by not less than ten qualified voters, residents of such township, city, town or ward; but the name of a candidate placed upon the ballot by any other method shall not be added by petition for the same office. Each elector so petitioning shall add to his signature his place of business and postoffice address. [24 G. A., ch. 33, § 5.]

Sec. 1101. Withdrawals. Any candidate named by either of the methods authorized in this chapter may withdraw his nomination by a written request, signed and acknowledged by him before any officer empowered to take the acknowledgment of deeds, and filed in the office of the secretary of state thirty days, or the proper auditor fifteen or clerk twelve days, before the day of election, and no name so withdrawn shall be printed upon the ballot. In case of a special election to fill vacancies in office, such withdrawal papers shall be filed with the secretary of state sixteen days, and with the proper auditor or clerk twelve days, before the day of such special election. [38 G. A., ch. 100; 36 G. A., ch. 245, § 1; 24 G. A., ch. 33, § 8.]

Sec. 1102. **Vacancies filled.** If a candidate declines a nomination, or dies before election day, or should any certificate of nomination or nomination paper be held insufficient or inoperative by the officer with whom it may be filed, or in case any objection made to any certificate of nomination, nomination paper, or to the eligibility of any candidate therein named, is sustained by the board appointed to determine such questions as hereinafter provided, the vacancy or vacancies thus occasioned may be filled by the convention, caucus, meeting or primary, or other persons making the original nominations, or in such a manner as such convention, caucus, meeting or primary has previously provided. If the time is insufficient for again holding such convention, caucus, meeting or primary, or. in case no such previous provisions being made, such vacancy shall be filled by the regularly elected or appointed executive or central committee of the particular division or district representing the political party or persons holding such convention, primary, meeting or caucus, and certified as hereinbefore provided. The certificates of nominations made to supply such vacancies shall state, in addition to the facts hereinbefore required, the name of the original nominee, the date of his death or declination of nomination, or the fact that the former nomination has been held insufficient or inoperative, and the measures taken in accordance with the above requirements for filling a vacancy, and shall be signed and sworn to by the presiding officer and secretary of the convention, caucus, meeting, or primary, or by the chairman and secretary of the committee, as the case may be. [24 G. A., ch. 33, § 9.]

Sec. 1104. **Filing certificates and petitions.** Certificates of nomination and nomination papers of candidates for state, congressional, judicial and legislative offices shall be filed with the secretary of state, not more than sixty nor less than forty days; those for all other officers, except for cities and towns, with the county auditors of the respective counties, not more than sixty nor less than thirty days; and for the offices in the cities and towns, with the clerks thereof, not more than forty nor less than fifteen days, before the day fixed by law for the holding of the election. Such certificates and nomination papers

thus filed, and being apparently in conformity with law, shall
be regarded as valid, unless objection in writing thereto shall
be made, and, under proper regulations, shall be open to public inspection, and preserved by the receiving officer for not less
than six months after the election is had. Any error found in
such papers may be corrected by the substitution of another,
executed as is required for an original nomination certificate or
paper. In case of special election to fill vacancies in office, certificates of nomination or nomination papers, for nomination of
candidates for office to be filled by the electors of a larger district than a county, may be filed with the secretary of state,
not later than fifteen days before the time of election. Certificates of nomination or nomination papers, nominating candidates for office to be filled by the electors of a county, may be
filed with the county auditor at any time not less than twelve
days before the election. [36 G. A., ch. 245, § 2; 26 G. A., ch.
68, §§ 1-2; 24 G. A., ch. 33, §§ 4, 7, 8, 10.]

DIVISION IX.

NOMINATION AND ELECTION OF JUDGES.

Chapter 63, Laws of the Thirty-eighth General Assembly.

Nomination and Election of Judges.

AN ACT to repeal sections one thousand eighty-seven-b (1087-b) one
thousand eighty-seven-b one (1087-b1), one thousand eighty-seven-b
two (1087-b2), one thousand eighty-seven-b three (1087-b3), one thousand eighty-seven-b four (1087-b4), one thousand eighty-seven-b five
(1087-b5), supplement to the code, 1913, and to enact a substitute
therefor, relating to the nomination and election of judges· of the
supreme, district and superior courts.

Be It Enacted by the General Assembly of the State of Iowa:

Section 1. **Repeal and substitute.** That the law as it appears in sections one thousand eighty-seven-b (1087-b), one
thousand eighty-seven-b one (1087-b1), one thousand eighty-
seven-b two (1087-b2), one thousand eighty-seven-b three
(1087-b3), one thousand eighty-seven-b four (1087-b4), one
thousand eighty-seven-b five (1087-b5), supplement to the
code, 1913, be and the same is hereby repealed, and the following enacted in lieu thereof.

Sec. 2. State judicial convention—delegates—organization —supreme court judges. A state judicial convention of each political party shall be held not less than one, nor more than two weeks, after the regular state convention of such party. Such state judicial convention shall convene at a time and place to be fixed by the state party committee, which shall issue a call therefor in the same manner that the call for the regular state convention is issued. Delegates to the state judicial convention shall be elected at, and certified by, the county conventions at the same time and in the same manner as delegates to the regular state convention, provided however, that no person shall be elected to act as delegate to both conventions; and each county shall be entitled to the same number of delegates at the state judicial convention as it is entitled to have at the regular state convention. The state judicial convention shall proceed to organize for the transaction of business in the same manner as is provided by law for the organization of the regular state convention and upon organization shall nominate candidates for the office of judge of the supreme court and may transact such other business as is proper. The method of procedure, organization and voting of delegates shall be the same in the state judicial convention as is provided for the regular state party convention. Judges of the supreme court shall be elected at the general election in November in the same manner as the governor of the state is elected.

Sec. 3. District central committee—how constituted—judicial convention—district court judges, etc. In each judicial district there shall be a district central committee composed of one member from each county of such district, provided, however, that in districts composed wholly of one county there shall be three members of such committee, and in districts composed of two counties there shall be two members of such committee from the county having the larger population. Such committeemen shall be selected by the county convention in each county held in accordance with the provisions of section ten hundred eighty-seven-a twenty-five (1087-a25), supplement to the code, 1913. Until such conventions are held, the chairman of the county central committee of each political party shall act as committeeman from his county for such judicial district, and in counties having more than one such committeeman such additional committeemen shall be selected by the county central committee in said county. Vacancies in any such district committee shall be filled by the county central committee of the county where such vacancy occurs. In each judicial district in which a judge, or judges, of the district court therein is to be elected, a judicial convention shall be held by each political party participating in the primary election of that year. Not less than ten days nor more than forty days before the day fixed for holding the county convention, a call for such judicial convention to be held shall be issued by the party central committee for such district, and published in at least one newspaper of general circulation in each county in the district which shall state, among other things, the number of delegates each county in the district shall be entitled to, and the time and place of holding the convention. Such call shall be filed with the county auditor in each county in the district not less than five days before the date of holding the county convention as now fixed by law, and the county auditor shall attach a copy thereof to the certified list of delegates required to be delivered by him to the chairman of the county central committee of the respective political parties. Each county convention held in such judicial district shall select such a number of delegates to the judicial convention as is specified in the call for such judicial convention. Such district convention shall not be held earlier than the first Thursday, nor later than the fifth Thursday following the date of holding the county convention. The convention may nominate as may candidates for the office of judge of the district court in said district as there are judges in said district to be elected at the general election to be held in the year in which such convention is held. The organization and the procedure in such judicial district convention shall be the same as in the state convention. Such convention may transact such other business as may properly be brought before it. Judges of the district court shall be elected at the general election in the same manner as state senators are elected.

Sec. 4. Supreme and district judges—certification of nomination—ballot form, etc. All nominations for the office of supreme and district judge shall be certified to the secretary of state, as near as may be, in the same manner that nominations for other state offices are now certified under existing law. The names of candidates for the office of supreme and district judge nominated and certified to the secretary of state, as provided in this act, shall be certified by the secretary of state, to the officer having charge of the printing of the ballots, and the names of such candidates shall be printed on the ballot under the proper party designation in the same manner as required by law for the printing of the names of candidates for state and district officers therein.

Sec. 5. **Judge of superior court—how nominated and elected.** In any city in which a superior court has been or may hereafter be established, the judge of said court shall be nominated and elected in the same manner now provided by law for the nomination and election of other elective officers in such city.

Sec. 7. **General election laws for state, etc., officers, applicable.** All the laws relating to the certificates of nomination, filing the same, certifying nominations to the officers having charge of the printing of the ballots, printing of the names of candidates on the official ballot, the method of withdrawal, filling vacancies, conducting general elections, of canvassing the ballot, of announcing the result, of recounting the ballot, of publishing notice of nomination and election, contesting the election, and the penalty for illegal voting, misconduct of the election officials, and the making of the sworn return, shall, so far as applicable, be the same for the election of supreme, district and superior judges as is now provided by the general election laws of Iowa for the election of state, district, county and city officers.

Sec. 6. **Nomination of judges by petition.** Nothing contained in this act shall be construed so as to prohibit the nominations of candidates for the office of supreme, district or superior judge, by petition as provided by section one thousand one hundred (1100) of the code, and amendments thereto, but no person so nominated shall be permitted to use the name of any political party authorized or entitled under this act to nominate candidates for such office.

DIVISION X.
REGISTRATION OF VOTERS.

Section 1076. **Board of registers—village precincts.** In cities having a population of six thousand or more, not including the inmates of any state institution, the council, on or before the sixth Monday preceding each general election, and on or before the third Monday prior to any city election to be held during the year nineteen hundred and six, shall appoint one suitable person from each of the two political parties which cast the greatest number of votes at the last general election, from three names presented by each chairman of the city central political committee of such parties, to be registers in each election precinct in the city for the registration of voters therein, who shall be electors of the precinct in which they are to serve, of good clerical ability, speaking the English language understandingly, temperate, of good habits and reputation, who shall qualify by taking an oath or affirmation to the effect that they will well and truly discharge all of the duties required of them by law. They shall hold their office for two years, but registers appointed for city elections during the year nineteen hundred and six shall hold such office only until such election is completed, and receive compensation at the rate of three dollars for each day of eight hours engaged in the discharge of their duties, to be paid by the county, except in case of city elections, when they shall be paid by the city. If for any cause such registers, or any of them, shall not be appointed at or before the time above mentioned, or, if appointed, shall be unable for any cause to discharge the duties of such office, the mayor of such city shall forthwith, on similar recommendation, make such appointments and fill all vacancies. Should the mayor, upon the request of five freehold electors, fail for a period of three days to perform the duties aforesaid, he shall forfeit and pay, at the action of any such elector, the sum of one hundred dollars per day, for the equal benefit of the city and plaintiff. The provisions of this title shall apply to cities acting under special charters, with like effect as though said cities were acting under the general incorporation laws of the state.

Provided further, that all cities in which registration is required, including cities under special charter, may, by resolution passed not less than thirty days or more than sixty days preceding any general, city or special election, consolidate the voting precincts of the city into registration districts for the purpose of registration only and appoint registrars for such registration districts; but such registrars must be residents and electors of the registration district in which they are to serve. [38 G. A., ch. 180; 37 G. A., ch. 41, § 1; 36 G. A., ch. 215, § 2; 35 G. A., ch. 108, §§ 1, 2; 31 G. A., ch. 41; 31 G. A., ch. 40, § 1; 26 G. A., ch. 62; 22 G. A., ch. 48, §§ 5, 12; 21 G. A., ch. 167, § 3.]

Sec. 1076-a. **Applicable to special charter cities.** This act shall apply to cities under special charters with same effect as to cities under the general laws. [31 G. A., ch. 40, § 2.]

Sec. 1085. **Notice.** The times and places of making registration of voters shall be published by the mayor in the two leading political party papers published in such city, except no publication shall be required for a special election. If there be but one such paper published in the city, publication of notice therein shall be sufficient. The publication shall be made for a period of three days prior to the opening of the registry book, if the paper is a daily paper, and for one week, if a weekly paper, and shall call the attention of the voters to the necessity of complying with the laws with reference to registration, in order to be entitled to vote at the ensuing election. [21 G. A., ch. 161, § 12.]

Sec. 1077. **Registration.** The registers shall meet on the second Thursday prior to any general, city, or special election, at the usual voting place in the precinct in which they have been appointed, and shall hold continuous sessions for two consecutive days, from eight o'clock in the forenoon until nine o'clock in the afternoon, and, in presidential years, such sessions shall be held for three days. Any person claiming to be a voter, or that he will be on election day, including women entitled to vote for president, vice president and presidential electors, may appear before them in the election precinct where he claims he is or will be entitled to vote, and make and subscribe, under oath, a statement in a registry book, to be provided by the clerk and furnished the registers, at the equal expense of the city and county, and kept open for public inspection and examination during the time fixed for the registration, which statement shall be in the following form and contain the following matter:

REGISTER OF VOTERS, ...PRECINCT, ...WARD.

Number	Residence	Name	Age	Nativity	Color	Precinct, street number	County	State	Naturalized	Date of Papers	Court	By act of Congress	Qualified Voter	Date of application	Last preceding place of residence	Signature
						Term of Residence										

The signature of the applicant shall be made at the right hand end of the line under the column "Signature," one of the registers having first administered to him this form of oath: "You do solemnly swear (or affirm) that you will fully and truly answer all such questions as shall be put to you touching. your place of residence, name, place of birth, your qualifications as an elector, and your right as such to register and vote under the laws of this state"; after which, the registers, or either of them, shall propound questions to the applicant for registration in relation to his name; his then place of residence, street and number; how long he has resided in the precinct where the vote is claimed; the last place of his residence before coming into that precinct; and also as to his citizenship, whether native or naturalized; if the latter, when, where, and in what court, or before what officer, or whether by act of congress; whether he came into the precinct for the purpose of voting at that election; how long he contemplates residing in the precinct; and such other questions as may tend to test his qualifications as a resident of the precinct, citizenship and right to vote at the poll; then, if the applicant appears to have the right to be registered, the registers shall fill out the above prescribed form of statement, which the applicant shall sign and swear to, as above provided. [38 G. A., ch. 353, § 4; 28 G. A., ch. 33, § 1; 22 G. A., ch. 48, § 1; 21 G. A., ch. 161, § 5.]

Sec. 1078. Statements—registry books—school elections. The statements thus made shall be dated and consecutively numbered, commencing with number one at each registration.

At the close of each day's registration, the registry book shall be ruled off so as to prevent further entries; and, when not in use by the registers, shall be kept in the custody of the clerk until disposed of as provided by law. No person shall register at any other place or time than is designated in this chapter, and no registration of voters for school elections shall be required. [22 G. A., ch. 48, § 10; 21 G. A., ch. 161, §§ 6, 8.]

Sec. 1079. List of voters. The registers shall, within three days after the registration made in the second week preceding the election, prepare two alphabetical lists, for their respective voting precincts, of the names of all persons registered, their residences, their last preceding places of residence, the dates of removal when removals occur within one year, nativity, color, term of residence in precinct, county and state, whether naturalized, date of papers, the naturalizing court, or place of naturalization if court is not known, whether naturalized by act of congress, date of application for registration; one of which lists they shall forthwith conspicuously post or cause to be posted at the usual place of holding elections in such precinct, for inspection of the public, and retain the other one in their possession. [22 G. A., ch. 48, § 12; 21 G. A., ch. 161, § 7.]

Sec. 1080. Correction of registry—lists delivered to judges. On the Saturday before any election at which registration is required, the registers shall meet at the place where registration was last made, and hold a continuous session, from eight o'clock in the forenoon until nine o'clock in the afternoon, at which they shall revise and correct the registry book of voters, adding thereto, consecutively numbering them, the names of all applying for registration who on election day will be entitled to vote in that precinct, and by striking therefrom the name of any one not entitled to vote thereat. The registers shall revise and correct the alphabetical list in their possession to correspond therewith. When thus revised and corrected, it shall be certified and copied by the registers, who shall deliver, or cause to be delivered, such list and copy to the judges of the election of the proper precinct, and which delivery shall be made on election day, and before the opening of the polls. The copy thus delivered shall be preserved by the judges, and returned with the vote from that precinct, and the original to the clerk. At the opening of the polls and before any ballot shall be received, the judges of the election shall appoint one of their number, or one of the clerks, to check the name of each voter whose name is on the alphabetical lists, to whom a ballot is delivered. [22 G. A., ch. 48, §§ 1, 3, 4; 21 G. A., ch. 161, § 8.]

Sec. 1081. **Appearance and hearing.** All proceedings of registers shall be public, and any person entitled to vote in a precinct shall have the right to be heard before them in reference to corrections of or additions to the lists of such precinct. No person shall be admitted to registry unless he appears in person, except as in this chapter provided, and, if demanded, he shall furnish to the registers such proofs of his right thereto as may by law be required by judges of election of any person offering to vote. If an elector is, by reason of sickness, unable to go to the place of registry on any day the registers may be in session, the registers shall, upon the filing before them, by a registered elector, of an affidavit to that effect, visit such sick elector at his place of residence on any day when not in session, and place his name on the registry book and alphabetical list, if found entitled thereto; at which time and place the registers may administer the oath hereinbefore provided to be taken by applicants for registry. [21 G. A., ch. 161, § 9.]

Sec. 1082. **Registration on election day.** The registers shall also be in session on the day for the holding of each election, at some place convenient to, but not within one hundred feet of, the voting place, and during all the hours in which by law the polls are required to be kept open, for the purpose only of granting certificates of registration to persons who, being electors, are not registered. Such registration shall be allowed and certificate thereof granted only to a person who was absent from the city during all the days fixed for registration of voters for that election, or to a person who, being a foreigner, has received his final papers since the last preceding day for the registration of voters for that election, or to a person whose name was, on the preceding Saturday, and in the absence of such person, stricken from registration, and who, on said day of election, shall prove to the satisfaction of said registers that he is a lawfully qualified elector of said voting precinct. These certificates of registration shall contain all the data showing the qualification of the voter as shown by the registration, and, in addition, the special matter showing the voter's right to such certificate under this section, and, before delivery to the applicant, shall be indorsed by the registers, to the effect that the person therein named is a qualified voter in that precinct, and that he is entitled to be registered as such. The proper statement shall be signed and sworn to by the voter before one of the registers, supported by the affidavit of a freeholder who is a registered voter in that precinct, who shall make oath to the qualification of the applicant as a voter in that precinct; and if the applicant be one whose name was stricken from registration, such affidavit of said freeholder shall contain the facts showing the right of said applicant to vote in that precinct. Registration in such cases shall be made in the manner required for regular registration. The certificate of registration shall be handed in to the judges of election when a ballot is delivered to him. The data therefrom, showing the voter's name and his qualification as a voter, shall be entered on the alphabetical lists by the judges and clerks of the election, under the appropriate headings, and the original certificate shall be returned to the city clerk, who shall carefully preserve it in the same manner and for the same time as the alphabetical list and poll book. [22 G. A., ch. 48, § 7.]

Sec. 1083. Striking off names. The registers, prior to each election except presidential elections, and after completing their registration, shall certify the names of all persons by them registered to the registers of the ward or precinct of the same city, which the registration shows such persons gave as their last place of residence, and the names of such persons so certified shall be stricken from the registry lists of the ward or precinct in which they last resided, if found thereon. [25 G. A., ch. 58, § 1.]

Sec. 1084. New registry—how often. A new registry of voters shall be taken in each year of a presidential election. For all other state or municipal elections, general or special, the registers shall prepare a new registry book in each year, by copying from the poll book of the preceding general election all the names found therein, adding thereto those of all persons registered and voting at any subsequent election, which new registry book shall show all the facts of qualification of each voter as they appear on the last preceding registry book, which, when thus made up, shall be used at each election until a new registry book is prepared as required by law. Every person thus registered shall be considered as entitled to vote at any election at which said registry book may be used, unless his name shall be dropped by the correction of registration, as authorized by law. [25 G. A., ch. 58, § 1; 22 G. A., ch. 48, §§ 2, 3.]

Sec. 1086. City clerk. The city clerk shall carefully preserve all registry books and alphabetical lists and other papers pertaining to the registration, until destroyed as provided in the chapter on the canvass of votes. He shall, on the application of the registers, deliver to them, prior to their first meeting for each election, the registry book, alphabetical list and poll book, which they require in order to properly prepare the necessary registry book for the next ensuing election; all of which shall be returned to him when they have completed their work for such election. [22 G. A., ch. 48, § 6.]

Sec. 1087. Penalty. If any register shall fail to perform any duty required of him in this chapter, he shall forfeit the sum of one hundred dollars, to be recovered by any person in any court having jurisdiction; and if any register or judge of election shall wilfully neglect or disregard any duty imposed, or shall make, or permit to be made, any registration, statement or list, except at the time and place and in the manner herein authorized and prescribed, or shall knowingly make, or permit to be made, any false statement as aforesaid, or if any person shall wilfully make, or authorize to be made, any statement required to be made, false in any particular, or shall violate any of the provisions of this chapter, every such register or judge of election, person or persons, shall be guilty of a misdemeanor, and, upon conviction, fined in a sum not less than fifty nor more than two hundred dollars, or be imprisoned in the county jail not less than twenty days, nor more than six months, or both, at the discretion of the court. [21 G. A., ch. 161, § 10.]

DIVISION XI.
METHOD OF CONDUCTING ELECTIONS.

Section 566. Places for holding elections. The trustees[1] shall designate the place where elections will be held, and the board of supervisors shall allow a reasonable compensation for the use thereof. Whenever a change is made from the usual place of holding elections in the township, notice of such change shall be given by posting up notices in three public places in the township, ten days prior to the day on which the election is to be held. [23 G. A., ch. 27; C. '73, § 391; R., § 444; C. '51, § 222.]

Sec. 1088. Elections included. The provisions of this chapter shall apply to all elections known to the laws of the state, except school elections. [21 G. A., ch. 141, § 2.]

Sec. 1089. General, city and special. The term "general election," as used in this chapter, shall apply to any election held for the choice of national, state, judicial, district, county or township officers; that of "city election" shall apply to any municipal election held in a city or town; and that of "special election" shall apply to any other election held for any purpose authorized or required by law. [24 G. A., ch. 33, § 2.]

Sec. 1090. Election precincts. Each township, or, in case a township contains a city or a portion thereof, such portion of the township as is outside the limits of the city, and each ward of a city, shall, respectively, constitute an election precinct. But the board of supervisors or the council, as the case may be, shall have power to divide a township or part thereof, or a ward, into two or more precincts, or to change or abolish the same; or the board of supervisors and the council of any city of less than thirty-five hundred inhabitants, not including the inmates of any state institution, may combine any part of the township outside of such city with any or all the wards thereof as one election precinct, or change or abolish such precinct; or the council of such city may combine the several wards into one or more precincts. No precinct shall contain different townships or parts thereof, except where by reason of the existence of a village or incorporated town on or near a township line, the board of supervisors may, for the convenience of electors, create a voting precinct in compact

---
[1]Township trustees.

form, from said town or village, and may include therein territory adjoining and adjacent to said village or town, which is situated in two or more townships. The board of supervisors in the order establishing such precinct shall define its boundaries and may change same if in their judgment occasion arises. In such cases, separate ballots and ballot boxes shall be provided for voting for township officers only. Each incorporated town shall constitute a precinct for town elections. No person shall vote in any precinct but that of his residence. [37 G. A., ch. 66; 33 G. A., ch. 70, § 1; 25 G. A., ch. 60; 21 G. A., ch. 141, § 2; C. '73, §§ 501, 603, 605; R., § 480; C. '51, § 245.]

Sec. 1091. Polling places for country precincts. Polling places for precincts outside the limits of a city, but within the township, or originally within and set off as a separate township from the township in which the city is in whole or in part situated, may, for the convenience of the voters, be fixed at some room or rooms in the courthouse or in some other building within the limits of the city as the board of supervisors may provide. [33 G. A., ch. 71, § 1; 21 G. A., ch. 161, § 14.]

Sec. 1092. Notice of boundaries of precincts. The board of supervisors or council shall number or name the several precincts established, and cause the boundaries of each to be recorded in the records of said board of supervisors or council, as the case may be, and publish notice thereof in some newspaper of general circulation, published in such county or city, once each week for three consecutive weeks, the last to be made at least thirty days before the next general election. The precincts thus established shall continue until changed. [C. '73, § 604.]

Sec. 1093. Election boards. Election boards shall consist of three judges and two clerks and their compensation shall be thirty cents per hour while engaged in the discharge of their duties. Not more than two judges and not more than one clerk shall belong to the same political party or organization, if there be one or more electors qualified and willing to act as such judge or clerk, and a member or members of opposite parties. In cities and towns, the councilmen shall be judges of election; but in case more than two councilmen belonging to the same political party or organization are residents of the same election precinct, the county board of supervisors may designate which of them shall serve as judges. In township precincts, the clerk of the township shall be a clerk of election of the precinct in which he resides, and the trustees of the township shall be judges of election, except that, in townships not divided into election precincts, if all the trustees be of the same political party, the board of supervisors shall determine by lot which two of the three trustees shall be judges of such precinct. The membership of such election board shall be made up or completed by the board of supervisors from the parties which cast the largest and next largest number of votes in said precinct at the last general election, or that one which is unrepresented; but, in city and town elections, the powers given in this chapter and duties herein made incumbent upon the board of supervisors shall be performed by the council. If, at the opening of the polls in any precinct, there shall be a vacancy in the office of clerk or judge of election, the same shall be filled by the members of the board present, and from the political party which is entitled to such vacant office under the provisions of this chapter. The election board at any special election shall be the same as at the last preceding general election. In case of vacancies happening therein, the county auditor may make the appointments to fill the same when the board of supervisors is not in session; providing, however. that the election board in precincts using only one voting machine shall consist of three judges, only two of whom shall be of the same political party, and two of whom shall also act as clerks.   [38 G. A., ch. 69; 36 G. A., ch. 215, § 3; 35 G. A., ch. 112, § 1; 31 G. A., ch. 42; 26 G. A., ch. 68, § 3; C. '73, §§ 606-8; R.. §§ 481-3; C. '51, §§ 246-8.]

Sec. 1113. Polling places—voting booths. In townships the trustees, and in cities and towns the mayor and clerk, shall provide suitable places in which to hold all elections provided for in this chapter, and see that the same are warmed, lighted, and furnished with proper supplies and conveniences, includ. ing a sufficient number or supply of booths, shelves, pens, penholders, ink, blotters and pencils to enable the voter to prepare his ballot for voting, screened from all observation as to the manner in which he does so. A guard rail shall be so constructed and placed that only such persons as are inside such rail can approach within six feet of the ballot box, or of the booths. The voting booths shall be so arranged that they can only be reached by passing within said guard rail, and so that they shall be in plain view of the election officers, and both booths and ballot boxes shall be in plain view of persons outside of the guard rail. Each booth shall be at least three feet square, and have three sides enclosed, the side in front to open and shut by a door swinging outward, or closed with a curtain. Each side of the booth shall be seven feet high, and the door or curtain shall extend to within two feet of the floor, and shall be closed while the voter is preparing his ballot. Each booth shall contain a shelf at least one foot wide, at a convenient height for writing, and shall be well lighted. The booths and compartments shall be so built and arranged, if possible, as to be permanent, so that after the election they may be taken down and deposited with the township, city or town clerk, as the case may be, for safekeeping and for future use. The number of voting booths shall not be less than one to every sixty voters or fraction thereof who voted at the last preceding election in the precinct. In precincts outside of cities and towns the election shall, if practicable, be held in the public school building, for the use of which there shall be no charge, but all damage to the building or furniture shall be paid by the county. [24 G. A., ch. 33, § 20.]

Sec. 1130. **Ballot boxes.** The board of supervisors shall provide for each precinct in the county, for the purpose of elections, one box, with lock and key. When any township precinct includes a town or part thereof, together with territory outside the limits of such town, the township trustees shall prepare a separate ballot box to receive the votes for township assessor, which shall be on separate ballots, and only the ballots of persons living outside of the limits of such town shall be placed in said ballot box. The judges of election shall place. each ballot in its proper ballot box. The judges of election shall have the right to administer an oath to any voter, and to examine him under oath as to the assessor for whom such elector is entitled to vote. [29 G. A., ch. 53, § 2; 17 G. A., ch. 71, §§ 2, 3; C. '73, § 614; R., § 489; C. '51, § 254.]

Sec. 1132. **Registry and poll books.** The county auditor shall prepare and furnish to each precinct two poll books, having each of them a sufficient column for the names of the voters, a column for the number, and sufficient printed blank leaves to contain the entries of the oaths, certificates and returns; and also all books, blanks and materials necessary to carry out the provisions of the chapter on registration of voters. [C. '73, § 615; R., § 490; C. '51, § 255.]

Sec. 1097. Voting by ballot. In all elections regulated by this chapter, the voting shall be by ballots printed and distributed as hereinafter provided, except as may be otherwise specially directed by law. [24 G. A., ch. 33, § 1.]

Sec. 1105. Nominations transmitted to county auditor. Not less than twenty days before the election, the secretary of state must certify to the auditor of each county in which any of the electors have the right to vote for any candidate or candidates, the name and residence of each person nominated, whether an original nomination or to fill a vacancy, to be voted for at such election, and the order in which the tickets shall appear on the ballot. Should a vacancy in the nominations occur and be filled after this certificate has been forwarded, a like certificate shall at once issue and be sent the proper officer. In case of special election to fill vacancy in office, the certificate by the secretary of state to the county auditor may be made at any time not later than fifteen days before the election. [36 G. A., ch. 245, § 3; 26 G. A., ch. 68, §§ 1, 2; 24 G. A., ch. 33, §§ 11-13.]

Sec. 1106. Ballot — form — presidential electors — United States senator—district judge—constitutional amendments— ballot for women. The names of all candidates to be voted for in such election precinct except electors of president and vice president of the United States shall be printed on one ballot, all nominations of any political party or group of petitioners being placed under the party name or title of such party or group, as designated by them in their certificates of nomination or petitions, or if none be designated, then under some suitable title, and the ballot shall contain no other names; provided, however, that the candidates for electors of president and vice president of any political party or group of petitioners shall not be placed on the ballot but in the years in which they are elected the names of candidates for president and vice president respectively of such parties or group of petitioners shall be placed on the ballot similarly, as the names of candidates for United States senators are placed thereon under their respective party, petition or adopted titles for each political party or group of petitioners nominating a set of candidates for electors, and upon the left-hand margin of each separate column of the ballot, immediately opposite the names of said candidates for president and vice president, a single square shall be printed in front of a bracket inclosing the names of the said candidates for president and vice president, and the votes for which candidates shall be counted and certified to by the election judges in the same manner as the votes for other candidates.

That at all general elections next preceding the expiration of the term of office of United States senator in the congress of the United States there shall be placed upon the official ballot in the proper place the names of candidates for all parties or group of petitioners for the office of United States senator that have been nominated by law and the votes for which candidates shall be counted and certified to by the election judges in the same manner as votes for other candidates.

Each list of candidates for the several parties and groups of petitioners shall be placed in a separate column on the ballot, in such order as the authorities charged with the printing of the ballots shall decide, except as otherwise provided, and be called a ticket. But the name of no candidate shall appear upon the ballot in more than one place for the same office, whether nominated by convention, primary, caucus or petition, except as hereinafter provided. Where two or more conventions, primaries or caucuses, or any two of them, may nominate the same candidate for any office, the name of such candidate shall be printed under the name of the party first filing nomination papers bearing such name, unless the candidate himself shall, in writing duly verified, request the officer with whom the nomination papers are filed to cause the name to be printed upon some other ticket, provided, that in any judicial district of the state in which the bar association, or a convention of attorneys of the district nominates or recommends candidate or candidates for the office of district judge, and such candidates are also nominated or indorsed by any political party, in preparing the ballots for the general election, the names of such candidate or candidates shall be printed as candidate or candidates for each party by whom they are nominated, whether by primary, convention or petition. Each of the columns containing the list of candidates, including the party name, shall be separated by a distance line. Said ballot shall be substantially in the following form:

○ REPUBLICAN	○ DEMOCRATIC	○ PROHIBITION	○ UNION LABOR
☐ { For President, A......... B........, of Ohio. For Vice President, C......... D........, of New York.	☐ { For President, N......... O........, of Virginia. For Vice President, P......... Q........, of Indiana.	☐ { For President, A......... B........, of Maine. For Vice President, C......... D........, of Illinois.	☐ { For President, N......... O........, of Idaho. For Vice President, P......... Q........, of Ohio.
For United States Senator,	For United States Senator,	For United States Senator,	For United States Senator,
☐ E......... F........, of.........County.	☐ R......... S........, of.........County.	☐ E......... F........, of.........County.	☐ R......... S........, of.........County.
For Governor,	For Governor,	For Governor,	For Governor,
☐ G......... H........, of.........County.	☐ T......... U........, of.........County.	☐ G......... H........, of.........County.	☐ T......... U........, of.........County.
For Lieutenant Governor,	For Lieutenant Governor,	For Lieutenant Governor,	For Lieutenant Governor,
☐ I......... J........, of.........County.	☐ V......... W........, of.........County.	☐ I......... J........, of.........County.	☐ V......... W........, of.........County.
For Judge of Supreme Court	For Judge of Supreme Court	For Judge of Supreme Court	For Judge of Supreme Court
☐ L......... M........, of.........County.	☐ X......... Y........, of.........County.	☐ L......... M........, of.........County.	☐ X......... Y........, of.........County.

When a constitutional amendment or other public measure is to be voted upon by the electors, it shall be printed in full upon a separate ballot, preceded by the words, "Shall the following amendment to the constitution (or public measure) be adopted?" and upon the right-hand margin, opposite these words, two spaces shall be left, one for votes favoring such amendment or public measure, and the other for votes opposing the same. In one of these spaces the word "yes" or other word required by law shall be printed; in the other, the word "no" or other word required, and to the right of each space a square shall be printed to receive the voting cross, all of which shall be substantially in the following form:

"Shall the following amendment to the constitution (or publice measure) be adopted?"

(Here insert in full the proposed constitutional amendment or public measure.)

Yes	
No	

The elector shall designate his vote by a cross mark, thus, X, placed in the proper square. At the top of such ballots shall be printed the following words, enclosed in brackets: [Notice to voters. For an affirmative vote upon any question submitted upon this ballot make a cross (x) mark in the square after the word "Yes." For a negative vote make a similar mark in the square following the word "No."] If more than one constitutional amendment or public measure is to be voted upon, they shall be printed upon the same ballot, one below the other, with one inch space between each constitutional amendment or public measure that is to be submitted. All of such ballots for the same polling place shall be of the same size, similarly printed, upon yellow colored paper. On the back of each such ballot shall be printed appropriate words, showing that such ballot relates to a constitutional or other question to be submitted to the electors, so as to distinguish the said ballots from the official ballot for candidates for office, and a facsimile of the signature of the auditor or other officer who has caused the ballot to be printed. Such ballots shall be endorsed and given to each voter by the judges of election, as provided in section eleven hundred sixteen, and shall be subject to all other laws governing ballots for candidates, so far as the same shall be applicable.

At any general election hereafter held for the election of presidential electors a separate ballot shall be provided for women, substantially in the following form:

O REPUBLICAN	O DEMOCRATIC	O PROHIBITION	O UNION LABOR
For President,	For President,	For President,	For President,
A.......... B.........,	N.......... O.........,	A.......... B.........,	N.......... O.........,
of Ohio.	of Virginia.	of Maine.	of Idaho.
For Vice President,	For Vice President,	For Vice President,	For Vice President,
C.......... D.........,	P.......... Q.........,	C.......... D.........,	P.......... Q.........,
of New York.	of Indiana.	of Illinois.	of Ohio.

And said ballot may be voted by them in the manner provided for the government of elections of said officers and shall be counted the same as other ballots cast at such elections. [38 G. A., ch. 353, § 2; 38 G. A., ch. 86, § 2; 35 G. A., ch. 109, § 4; 31 G. A., chs. 43-44; 28 G. A., ch. 35, § 1; 24 G. A., ch. 33, §§ 14, 16.]

Sec. 56. Submission of constitutional amendments to vote —results declared—record. Whenever a proposition to amend the constitution shall have been adopted by two succeeding general assemblies, if no other time is fixed by the last general assembly adopting the same for its submission to the people, it shall be done at the ensuing general election, in the manner required by law, and the board of state canvassers shall declare the result and enter the same of record in the book mentioned in the preceding section[1], immediately following and in connection with the proofs of publication.[2] [19 G. A., ch. 7, § 1; 16 G. A., ch. 144, § 2.]

Sec. 58. **Submission at special election.** The general assembly may provide for the submission of constitutional amendments to the people at a special election for that purpose, at such time as it may prescribe, proclamation for which election shall be made by the governor, and the same shall in all respects be governed and conducted as prescribed by law for the submission of constitutional amendments at a general election. [19 G. A., ch. 7, § 2.]

Sec. 1107. **Printing.** For all elections held under this chapter, except those of cities or towns, the county auditor shall have charge of the printing of ballots in his county, and shall cause to be placed thereon the names of all candidates which have been certified to him by the secretary of state, in the order the same appear upon the certificate issued by the secretary of state, together with those of all other candidates to be voted for thereat, whose nominations have been made in conformity with law. If a township election precinct includes a town or any part thereof, the names of nominees for township assessors shall not be placed upon the official ballot for that precinct. In no case shall the cost of printing the official ballot exceed twenty-five dollars per thousand ballots, except in presidential years, when it shall not exceed thirty dollars per thousand ballots. In city or town elections, the clerk shall have charge of the printing of the ballots, and shall cause to be placed thereon the names of all candidates to be voted for thereat, whose nominations have been made as provided in this chapter; and in either case such ballots shall be furnished the election judges at the polling place in each precinct not less than twelve hours before the opening of the polls on the morning of the election. [36 G. A., ch. 239; 24 G. A., ch. 33, § 15.]

Sec. 1109. **Method of printing.** The ballot shall be on plain white paper, through which the printing or writing cannot be read. The party name or title shall be printed in capital letters, not less than one-fourth of an inch in height. The names of candidates shall be printed in capital letters not less than one-eighth nor more than one-fourth of an inch in height, and, at the beginning of each line in which the name of a candidate is printed, a square shall be printed, the sides of which shall not be less than one-fourth of an inch in length. On the back or outside of the ballot, so as to.appear when folded, shall be printed the words "official ballot," followed by the designation of the polling place for which the ballot is prepared, the date of the election, and a facsimile of the signature of the auditor or other officer who has caused the ballot to be printed. [31 G. A., ch. 44, §2; 24 G. A., ch. 33, §14.]

Sec. 1108. Vacancies filled. The name supplied for a vacancy by the certificate of the secretary of state, or by nomination certificates or papers for a vacancy filed with the county auditor, or city or town clerk, shall, if the ballots are not already printed, be placed on the ballots in place of the name of the original nominee, or, if the ballots have been printed, new ballots, whenever practicable, shall be furnished. Whenever it may not be practicable to have new ballots printed, the election officers having charge of them shall place the name supplied for the vacancy upon each ballot used before delivering it to the judges of election. If said ballots have already been delivered to the judges of election, said auditor or clerk shall immediately furnish the name of such substituted nominee to all judges of election within the territory in which said nominee may be a candidate, and such election officer having charge of the ballots shall place the name supplied for the vacancy upon each ballot issued before delivering it to the voter, by affixing a paster, or by writing or stamping the name thereon. [24 G. A., ch. 33, §§ 11, 12.]

Sec. 1110. Delivery of official ballots to judges. Ballots shall be printed and in the possession of the officer charged with their distribution at least two days before the election, and subject to the inspection of candidates and their agents. If mistakes are discovered, they shall be corrected without delay, in the manner provided in this chapter. The officers charged with the printing of the ballots shall cause to be delivered to the judges of election seventy-five ballots, of the kind to be voted in such precinct, for every fifty votes or fraction thereof cast therein at the last preceding election of state officers. Such ballots shall be put up in separate sealed packages, with marks on .the outside, clearly designating the polling place for which they are intended and the number of ballots inclosed, and receipt therefor shall be given by the judge or judges of election to whom they are delivered, which receipt shall be preserved by the officer charged with the printing of the ballots. Any officer charged with the printing and distribution of ballots shall provide and retain at his office an ample supply of ballots, in addition to those distributed to the several voting precincts, and if at any time the ballots furnished to any precinct shall be lost, destroyed or exhausted before the polls are closed, on written application, signed by a majority of the judges of such precinct, or signed and sworn to by one of such judges, he shall immediately cause to be delivered to such judges, at the polling place, such additional supply of ballots as may be required, and sufficient to comply with the provisions of this chapter. For general elections, the supply of ballots so retained shall only equal the number provided for the precinct casting the largest vote at the preceding general election, and shall include only the portions of the various tickets to be voted for throughout the entire county, with blank spaces in which the names of candidates omitted may be written by the voter, and with blank spaces in the indorsement upon the back of such ballots, in which the name of the precinct shall be written by the judges of election. [24 G. A., ch. 33, §15.]

Sec. 1111. Card of instructions. The officer whose duty it is to have the ballots printed shall cause to be copied upon cards in large, clear type, under the heading "Card of Instructions," the following matters for the guidance of the voters:

1. The matter of obtaining ballots.

2. The manner of marking ballots.

3. That unmarked or improperly marked ballots will not be counted.

4. The method of gaining assistance in marking ballots.

5. That any erasures or identification marks, or otherwise spoiling or defacing a ballot, will render it invalid.

6. Not to vote a spoiled or defaced ballot.

7. How to obtain a new ballot in place of a spoiled or defaced one.

8. Upon the right of an employe to absent himself for two hours for the purpose of voting, by application for leave so to do made before the day of election, without deduction from his salary or wages.

9. Any other matters thought necessary.

Such instructions shall be prepared by the attorney general and delivered to the secretary of state, who shall cause copies of the same to be furnished to the county auditor of each county. New or amended instructions may be so prepared from time to time, if thought necessary, and copies thereof furnished to the county auditors, who shall furnish to the judges of election a sufficient number of such cards of instruction as will enable them to comply with the provisions of this chapter. [24 G. A., ch. 33, § 17.]

Sec. 1112. Cards posted—publication of ballot. The judges of election shall cause at least one of each of such cards to be posted in each voting booth or apartment provided for the preparation of ballots, and not less than four, with an equal number of sample ballots, in and about the polling place, upon the day of election before the opening of the polls. The county auditor shall cause to be published, prior to the day of election, in two newspapers, if there be so many published in such county, selecting, if possible, papers representing the political parties which cast at the preceding general election the largest number and the next largest number of votes, a list of all the nominations made, as herein provided, and to be voted for at such election, as near as may be in the form in which they shall appear upon the general ballot, but such publication shall not include portions of the ballot relating to township, city or town officers. [24 G. A., ch. 33, § 18.]

Sec. 1096. Polls open. At all elections the polls shall be opened at eight o'clock in the forenoon, except in cities where registration is required, when the polls shall be opened at seven o'clock in the forenoon, or in each case as soon thereafter as vacancies in the places of judges or clerks of election have been filled. In all cases the polls shall be closed at seven o'clock in the evening. [28 G. A., ch. 34, § 1; 24 G. A., ch. 33, § 32; C. '73, § 611; R., § 486; C. '51, § 251.]

Sec. 1094. Oath. Before opening the polls, each of the judges and clerks shall take the following oath: "I, A. B., do solemnly swear that I will impartially, and to the best of my knowledge and ability, perform the duties of judge (or clerk) of this election, and will studiously endeavor to prevent fraud, deceit and abuse in conducting the same." [C. '73, § 609; R., § 484; C. '51, § 249.]

Sec. 1095. **How administered.** Any one of the judges or clerks present may administer the oath to the others, and it shall be entered in the poll books, subscribed by the person taking it, and certified by the officer administering it. [C. '73, § 610; R., § 485; C. '51, § 250.]

Sec. 1114. **Ballot furnished to voter.** The judges of election of their respective precincts shall have charge of the ballots and furnish them to the voters. Any person desiring to vote shall give his name, and, if required, his residence, to such judges, one of whom shall thereupon announce the same in a loud and distinct tone of voice, clear and audible. In precincts where registration is required, if such name is found on the register of voters by the officer having charge thereof, he shall likewise repeat such name in the same manner; if the name of the person desiring to vote is not found on the register of voters, his ballot shall not be received until he shall have complied with the law prescribing the manner and conditions of voting by unregistered voters. [24 G. A., ch. 33, § 19.]

Sec. 1115. **Challenges.** Any person offering to vote may be challenged as unqualified by any judge or elector; and it is the duty of each of the judges to challenge any person offering to vote whom he knows or suspects not to be duly qualified; and he shall not receive a ballot from a voter who is challenged, until such voter shall have established his right to vote. When any person is so challenged, the judges shall explain to him the qualifications of an elector, and may examine him under oath touching his qualifications as a voter. In all precincts where registration is not required, and in other precincts where the name of such voter is entered upon the registration lists, if the person challenged insists that he is qualified, and the challenge is not withdrawn, one of the judges shall tender to him the following oath: "You do solemnly swear that you are a citizen of the United States, that you are a resident good faith of this precinct, that you are twenty-one years of age as you verily believe, that you have been a resident of this county sixty days, and of this state six months next pre-

ceding this election, and that you have not voted at this election," and if he takes such oath, his vote shall be received.
[24 G. A., ch. 33, § 21; C. '73, §§ 619, 620; R., §§ 493-4; C. '51,
§§ 258-9.]

Sec. 1116. **Method of voting.** Any voter entitled to receive
a ballot under the provisions of this chapter shall be allowed to
enter the space inclosed by the guard rail. One of the judges
shall give him one, and only one, ballot, on the back of which
such judge shall indorse his initials, in such manner that they
may be seen when the ballot is properly folded, and the voter's
name shall immediately be checked on the registry list. The
name of each person, when a ballot is delivered to him, shall be
entered by each of the clerks of election in the poll book kept
by him, in the place provided therefor. [24 G. A., ch. 33, § 21;
C. '73, § 621; R., § 495; C. '51, § 260.]

Sec. 1117. **Depositing ballot.** On receipt of the ballot, the
voter shall, without leaving the inclosed space, retire alone to
one of the voting booths, and without delay mark his ballot,
and, before leaving the voting booth, shall fold the same in
such manner as to conceal the marks thereon, and deliver the
same to one of the judges of election, but the number of the
voter on the poll books or register lists shall not be indorsed on
the back of his ballot. One of the judges of election shall
thereupon, in the presence of the voter, deposit such ballot in
the ballot box, but no ballot without the official indorsement
shall be allowed to be deposited therein. The voter shall quit
said inclosed space as soon as he has voted. Any voter who,
after receiving an official ballot, decides not to vote, shall, before retiring from within the guard rail, surrender to the election officers the official ballot which has been given him, and
such fact shall be noted on each of the poll lists. A refusal to
surrender such ballot shall subject the person so offending to
immediate arrest and the penalties provided in this chapter.
No voter shall vote or offer to vote any ballot except such as he
has received from the judges of election in charge of the ballots. No person shall take or remove any ballot from the polling place before the close of the poll. No voter shall be allowed
to occupy a voting booth already occupied by another nor remain within said inclosed space more than ten minutes, nor
to occupy a voting booth more than five minutes, in case all of
said voting booths are in use and other voters waiting to occu-

py the same, nor to again enter the inclosed space after having voted; nor shall more than two voters in excess of the whole number of voting booths provided be allowed at any one time in such inclosed space, except by the authority of the election officers to keep order and enforce the law. [24 G. A., ch. 33, §§ 20-2, 25; C. '73, § 617; R., § 492; C. '51, § 257.]

Sec. 1118. **Assistance to vote.** Any voter who may declare upon oath that he cannot read the English language, or that, by reason of any physical disability, he is unable to mark his ballot, shall, upon request, be assisted in marking the same by two of the election officers of different political parties, to be selected from the judges and clerks of the precinct in which they are to act, to be designated by the judges of election of each precinct at the opening of the polls. Such officers shall mark the ballot as directed by the voter, and shall thereafter give no information regarding the same. The clerks of election shall enter upon the poll lists, after the name of any elector who received such assistance in marking his ballot, a memorandum of the fact. Intoxication shall not be regarded as a physical disability, and no intoxicated person shall be entitled to assistance in marking his ballot. [24 G. A., ch. 33, § 23.]

Sec. 1119. **Marking the ballot.** Upon retiring to the voting booth the voter shall mark his ballot. He may place a cross, if he desires, in the circle at the head of one ticket on the ballot and the voter may place a cross in the square opposite the name of any candidate for whom he desires to vote, whether he has put a cross in the circle or not.

If the voter does not wish to vote for all the candidates of his party to an office where more than one candidate is to be elected, the cross in the circle at the top of his ticket shall not apply to said office, but the voter must mark crosses in the squares opposite the names of the candidates for whom he intends to vote. The voter may also insert in writing in the proper place the name of any person for whom he desires to vote, making a cross opposite thereto. The writing of such name without making a cross opposite thereto, or the making of a cross in a square opposite a blank without writing a name therein shall not affect the validity of the vote. [38 G. A., ch. 86, § 7; 31 G. A., ch. 44, § 3; 28 G. A., ch. 36, § 1; 24 G. A., ch. 33, § 22.]

Sec. 1120. Ballot — marking for candidate — rejection. When a circle is marked the ballot shall be counted for all the candidates upon the ticket beneath said circle, except those offices for which some candidate has been voted for by marking a square. A cross placed in a square shall be counted for the candidate before whose name the square is so marked.

When a square in front of any candidate has been marked, a mark in the circle shall not count for any candidate for that particular office. When more candidates than the number to be elected to the same office are voted for. by marking the squares opposite their names the vote shall not be counted for any candidate for that office. If less than the whole number of candidates to be elected are voted for by marking the squares opposite their names the vote shall be counted only for those marked in the square and the mark in the circle shall not apply. If for any reason it is impossible to determine the voter's choice for any office, his ballot shall not be counted for such office, but a mark in the circle of any ticket on the ballot shall not be held to make it impossible to determine the voter's choice. Any ballot marked by the voter in any other manner than as authorized in this chapter, and so that such mark may be used for the purpose of identifying such ballot shall be rejected. [38 G. A., ch. 86, § 8; 31 G. A., ch. 44, § 4; 24 G. A., ch. 33, §§ 22, 27.]

Sec. 1121. Voting mark—spoiled ballots. The voting mark shall be a cross in the square opposite to the name of the candidate for whom the voter desires to vote. Any voter who shall spoil his ballot may, on returning the same to the judges, receive another in place thereof, but no voter shall receive more than three ballots, including the one first delivered to him. None. but ballots provided in accordance with the provisions of this chapter shall be counted. [31 G. A., ch. 44, § 5; 24 G. A., ch. 33, §§ 22, 25.]

Sec. 1122. Defects in printed ballot. No ballot properly marked by the voter shall be rejected because of any discrepancy between the printed ballot and the nomination paper or certificate of nomination, and it shall be counted for the candidate or candidates for such offices named in the nomination paper or certificate of nomination. No ballot furnished by the proper officer shall be rejected for any error in stamping or writing the indorsements thereon by the officials charged with such duties, nor because of any error on the part of the officer charged with such duty in delivering the wrong ballots at any precinct or polling place, but any ballot delivered by the proper official to any voter shall, if properly marked by the voter, be counted as cast for all candidates for whom the voter had the right to vote, and for whom he has voted.

Sec. 1131. **Voting by women.** At all elections where women may vote, no registration of women shall be required; separate ballots shall be furnished for the question on which they are entitled to vote; a separate ballot box shall be provided in which all ballots cast by them shall be deposited, and a separate canvass thereof made by the judges of the election, and the returns thereof shall show such vote; except that in elections for president, vice president and presidential electors, women shall be required to register as provided in chapter two (2) of this title,[1] and acts amendatory thereto, and separate ballot box shall not be used for women's ballots at such elections. The right of any citizen to vote at any city, town or school election, on the question of issuing any bonds for municipal or school purposes, and for the purpose of borrowing money, or on the question of increasing the tax levy, shall not be denied or abridged on account of sex. [38 G. A., ch. 353, § 3; 25 G. A., ch. 39.]

Sec. 1124. **Persons at polling place.** No persons shall, during the receiving and counting of the ballots at any polling place, loiter, or congregate, or do any electioneering or soliciting of votes, within one hundred feet of any outside door of any building affording access to any room where the polls are held, or of any outside door of any building affording access to any hallway, corridor, or stairway, or other means of reaching such room, nor shall any person interrupt, hinder or oppose any voter while approaching or leaving the polling place for the purpose of voting; but any person who is by law authorized to perform or is charged with the performance of official duties at the election, and any number of persons, not exceeding three from each political party having candidates to be voted for at such election, to act as challenging committees, who are appointed and accredited by the executive or central committee of such political party or organization, respectively, or of persons not exceeding three from each of such political

---

[1]See sec. 1077, supra.

parties, appointed and accredited in the same manner as above prescribed for challenging committees, to witness the counting of ballots, may be present at the polling place. [24 G. A., ch. 33, § 26; 22 G. A., ch. 48, § 9; 21 G. A., ch. 161, § 13.]

Sec. 1128. **Arrest of disorderly persons.** If any person conducts himself in a noisy, riotous, tumultuous or disorderly manner at or about the polls, so as to disturb the election, or insults or abuses the judges or clerks of election, or commits a breach of the peace, or violates any of the provisions of this chapter, the judges or clerks of the election, or any of them, shall order the arrest of any such person, and the constable or any special policeman may forthwith arrest him and bring him before the judges of election, and they, by a warrant under their hands, may commit him to the jail of the county for a term not exceeding twenty-four hours, but they shall permit him to vote. [22 G. A., ch. 48, § 9; 21 G. A., ch. 161, § 13; C. '73, § 613; R., § 488; C. '51, § 253.]

Sec. 1134. **Interference with voters.** No person shall on election day do any electioneering or solicit votes within any polling place, or within one hundred feet therefrom, as defined in this chapter, or interrupt, hinder or oppose any voter while approaching the polling place for the purpose of voting; nor shall any voter, except as provided by law, allow his ballot to be seen by any person, or make a false statement as to his inability to mark his ballot; nor shall any person interfere or attempt to interfere with any voter when inside the inclosed space, or when marking his ballot, or endeavor to induce any voter, before voting, to show how he marks or has marked his ballot; nor shall any person mark, or cause in any manner to be marked, on any ballot any character for the purpose of identifying such ballot. Any violation of the provisions of this section shall be punished by a fine of not less than five nor more than one hundred dollars, or by imprisonment for not less than ten days nor more than thirty days in the county jail, or by both fine and imprisonment. [24 G. A., ch. 33, §§ 26, 27.]

Sec. 1123. **Employes.** Any person entitled to vote at a general election shall, on the day of such election, be entitled to absent himself from any services in which he is then employed for a period of two hours, between the time of opening and closing the polls, which period may be designated by the employer, and such voter shall not be liable to any penalty, nor shall any deduction be made from his usual salary or wages, on account of such absence, but application for such absence shall be made prior to the day of election. Any employer who shall refuse to an employe the privilege, conferred by this section, or shall subject such employe to a penalty or reduction of wages because of the exercise of such privilege, or shall in any manner attempt to influence or control such employe as to how he shall vote, by offering any reward, or threatening discharge from employment, or otherwise intimidating or attempting to intimidate such employe from exercising his right to vote, shall be punished by a fine of not less than five nor more than one hundred dollars. [24 G. A., ch. 33, § 24.]

Sec. 1135. **Defacing posted lists or cards.** Any person who shall, prior to any election, wilfully destroy or deface any list of candidates posted in accordance with the provisions of this chapter, or who, during an election, shall wilfully deface, tear down, remove or destroy any card of instruction or specimen ballot printed and posted for the instruction of voters, or who shall, during an election, wilfully remove or destroy any of the supplies or conveniences furnished to enable voters to prepare their ballots, or shall wilfully hinder the voting of others, shall be punished by a fine of not less than ten nor more than one hundred dollars, or imprisonment for not less than ten nor more than thirty days, or by both fine and imprisonment. [24 G. A., ch. 33, § 28.]

Sec. 1137. **Official neglect or misconduct.** Any public officer upon whom a duty is imposed by this chapter, who shall wilfully neglect to perform such duty, or who shall wilfully perform it in such a way as to hinder the object thereof, or shall disclose to any one, except as may be ordered by any court of justice, the contents of any ballot, as to the manner in which the same may have been voted, shall be punished by a fine of not less than five nor more than one thousand dollars, or by imprisonment in the penitentiary for not less than one nor more than five years, or by both fine and imprisonment. [24 G. A., ch. 33, § 30.]

Sec. 1125. **Special policemen.** The city council shall detail and employ, on the nomination of the principal political committee of each political party recognized as the two leading parties, from citizens, or the police force of the city, from two to four special policemen for each precinct, and fully empower them for the special occasion of each election, who shall be men of good character and reputation, in equal numbers from each of the leading political parties, to prevent the violation of any of the terms, provisions or requirements of this chapter, or of any other command made in pursuance of any provisions hereof, and no other peace officer than those above named shall exercise his authority for preserving order at or within one hundred feet of such voting places, unless called in by an emergency. If no policeman be in attendance, the judges of election may appoint one or more specially, by writing, who shall have all the powers of such special policeman. [22 G. A., ch. 48, § 9; 21 G. A., ch. 161, § 13.]

Sec. 1126. Constables. Except in voting precincts within any city, any constable of the township, who may be designated by the judges of election, shall attend at the place of election; if none attend, the judges of the election may, in writing, specially appoint one or more, who shall have all the powers of a regular constable. [C. '73, § 612; R., § 487; C. '51, § 252.]

Sec. 1127. Preserving order. All special policemen and constables are authorized and required to preserve order and peace at all places of election, and such special policemen, constables, and all other persons are authorized and required to obey the lawful orders and commands of said judges of election given to prevent violations of this chapter. [22 G. A., ch. 48, § 9; 21 G. A., ch. 161, § 13; C. '73, § 612; R., § 487; C. '51, § 252.]

Sec. 1129. Expenses — special policemen — compensation. The special policemen appointed under the provisions of this chapter shall be entitled to receive two dollars a day as compensation for their services, which with the expense of providing booths, guard rails, and other things required in this chapter shall be paid in the same manner as other election expenses. The printing and distributing of ballots and cards of instruction to the voters, described in this chapter, for any general election, shall be at the expense of the county, and shall be provided for in the same manner as other county election expenses. The printing and distribution of ballots for use in city elections shall be at the expense of the city or town in which the election shall be held. [30 G. A., ch. 39; 24 G. A., ch. 33, §§ 2, 20.]

Sec. 1133. Penalty. Any person violating or attempting to violate any provisions or requirements of this chapter, or failing or refusing to comply with any order or command of an election officer, made in pursuance of the provisions of this chapter, shall be punished by a fine of not less than fifty, nor more than two hundred dollars, or by imprisonment of not less than twenty days, nor more than six months, in the county jail. [22 G. A., ch. 48, § 9; 21 G. A., ch. 161, § 13.]

Sec. 1134-a. **Promise of position prohibited.** It shall be unlawful for any candidate for any office to be voted for at any primary, municipal or general election, prior to his nomination or election, to promise, either directly or indirectly, to support or use his influence in behalf of any person or persons for any position, place or office, or to promise directly or indirectly to name or appoint any person or persons to any place, position or office in consideration of any person or persons supporting him or using his, her or their influence in securing his or her nomination, election or appointment. [35 G. A., ch. 303, § 1.]

Sec. 1134-b. **Promise of influence prohibited.** It shall be unlawful for any person to solicit from any candidate for any office to be voted for at any primary, municipal or general election, or any candidate for appointment to any public office, prior to his nomination, election or appointment, to promise, directly or indirectly, to support or use his or her influence in behalf of any person or persons for any position, place or office, or to promise either directly or indirectly to name or appoint any person or persons to any place, position or office in consideration of any person or persons supporting him or her, or using his, her or their influence in securing his or her nomination, election or appointment. [35 G. A., ch. 303, § 2.]

Sec. 1134-c. **Penalty.** Any person violating any of the provisions of this act shall be deemed guilty of a misdemeanor and punished as provided in section eleven hundred thirty-seven-a six, supplement to the code, 1907. [35 G. A., ch. 303, § 3.]

DIVISION XII.
CANVASS OF VOTES.

Section 1138. **By judges.** When the poll is closed, the judges of election shall forthwith, and without adjournment, canvass the vote and ascertain the result of it, comparing the poll lists and correcting errors therein. Each clerk shall keep a tally list of the count. The canvass shall be public, and each

6. Senators and representatives in the general assembly by districts comprising more than one county.

7. Judges of the district court.

8. County officers.

9. Senators in the congress of the United States. [38 G. A., ch. 86, § 3; C. '73, §§ 636, 662; R., §§ 507, 538-9; C. '51, §§ 272, 304-5.]

Sec. 1151. Duplicate abstracts. Abstracts of all the votes cast for senators in the congress of the United States, congressmen, president and vice president of the United States, state or judicial district officers, shall be made in duplicate, and signed by the board of county canvassers, one of which shall be forwarded to the secretary of state, and the other filed by the county auditor. [38 G. A., ch. 86, § 4; C. '73, §§ 637, 662; R., §§ 507, 538-9; C. '51, §§ 272, 304-5.]

Sec. 1152. Declaration of election. Each abstract of the votes for such officers as the county alone elects shall contain a declaration of whom the canvassers determined to be elected, except when two or more persons receive an equal and the greatest number of votes. [C. '73, § 639; R., § 509; C. '51, § 275.]

Sec. 1153. For senator or representative for district. When a senator or representative in the general assembly is elected by a district composed of two or more counties, the several boards of canvassers therein shall, after the canvass of the vote, make and certify as many copies of the abstract of the votes for such office as there are counties in such senatorial or representative district, and one additional, and the auditor in each county shall seal up, direct and transmit one copy to the secretary of state, and one to the auditor of each other county in the district, who shall file the same in their respective offices, and he shall preserve one in his office. [C. '73, § 646.]

Sec. 1154. Returns filed. When the canvass is concluded, the board shall deliver the original returns to the auditor, who shall file the same, and record each of the abstracts above mentioned in the election book. [C. '73, § 640; R., §§ 335, 510; C. '51, § 276.]

Sec. 1155. Certificate of election. When any person is thus declared elected, there shall be delivered him a certificate of election, under the official seal of the county, in substance as follows:

STATE OF IOWA, }
.................County. }

At an election holden in said county on the............day of............................,........,
A. D............, A.................B.................was elected to the office of..................
of the said county for the term of.................years from the.................day
of................, A. D.............., (or if he was elected to fill a vacancy, say for the residue of the term ending on the.................day of
................................, A. D..............), and until his successor is
elected and qualified.

C.................D........................,
President of Board of Canvassers.

Witness, E.................F................., County Auditor (Clerk).

which certificate shall be presumptive evidence of his election
and qualification. [C. '73, § 641; R., §§ 511, 514; C. '51, § 277.]

Sec. 1156. **Of senators and representatives.** The certificate
of election of senators and representatives shall be in duplicate, and substantially in the form given, with such changes
only as are necessary, one of which shall be delivered to the
person entitled thereto, and the other forwarded to the secretary of state. [C. '73, § 642; R., § 512; C. '51, § 278.]

Sec. 1157. Abstracts forwarded to secretary of state.
Within ten days after the election, one of the abstracts of votes
for governor and lieutenant governor shall be sealed up by the
auditor, indorsed "Abstract of votes for governor and lieutenant governor from.................county (naming the county),"
and be by him forwarded to the speaker of the house of representatives; those for president and vice president of the
United States, senators and representatives in congress, and
all other state and district officers, shall be separately sealed
up, indorsed in like manner, with necessary changes, and then
all placed in one package and forwarded to the secretary of
state. Abstracts of votes cast at special elections to fill vacancies in office shall be forwarded as soon as canvassed. [38 G.
A., ch. 86, § 5; 35 G. A., ch. 109, § 7; C. '73, §§ 645, 662; R.,
§§ 517, 518, 538-9; C. '51, §§ 283-4, 304-5.]

Sec. 1158. **Returns procured from counties.** If the abstracts from any county are not received at the office of the
secretary of state within fifteen days after the day of election,
he shall send a messenger to the auditor of such county, who
shall furnish him with them, or, if they have been sent, with
a copy thereof, and he shall return them to the secretary without delay. [C. '73, §§ 649, 662; R., §§ 519, 538-9; C. '51,
§§ 285, 304-5.]

Sec. 30-a. Canvass of votes—oath—message of governor. The general assembly shall meet in joint session on the second Tuesday of January or as soon thereafter as both houses have been organized after the biennial election, and canvass the votes cast for governor and lieutenant governor and determine the election; and when the canvass is completed, the oath of office shall be administered to the persons so declared elected and the governor shall deliver to the joint assembly any message he may deem expedient. [35 G. A., ch. 2, § 1.]

Sec. 1159. Abstracts opened. The abstracts received by the secretary of state shall be kept by him until the day fixed for their opening, and shall then be opened only in the presence of the state board of canvassers. [C. '73, § 650; R., § 520; C. '51, § 286.]

Sec. 1160. State board of canvassers. The executive council constitutes a board of canvassers for the state, but no member thereof shall take part in canvassing the votes for any office for which he himself is a candidate. [C. '73, § 651; R., § 521; C. '51, § 287.]

Sec. 1161. Time of state canvass. On the twentieth day after the day of election, the board of state canvassers shall open and examine all of the returns. If they are not received from all the counties, it may adjourn, not exceeding twenty days, for the purpose of obtaining them, and, when received, shall proceed with the canvass. Returns of elections to fill vacancies in office shall be canvassed as soon as received. [C. '73, §§ 652, 663; R., §§ 522, 540; C. '51, §§ 288, 306.]

Sec. 1162. Canvass by state board, including votes for United States senator. The board of state canvassers shall open the abstracts for state senators and representatives transmitted to the secretary of state, and canvass the votes therein returned, at the time and in the manner of canvassing the state vote, or at such other time as they may fix, at least twenty days prior to the time fixed by law for the meeting of the next general assembly, and in case of a special election, within five days after the receipt of such abstracts, and shall immediately make out, certify, and transmit by mail to the county auditor of each county in the district, to be by him filed in his office, a copy of the abstract of such canvass required in the next section, which shall be recorded by him in the election book. The said board shall at the same time and in the same manner open the abstracts of the vote for senator in the congress of the United States, transmitted to the secretary of state, and canvass the vote therein returned.* [35 G. A., ch. 109, § 8; C. '73, § 647.]

Sec. 1163. Abstract of result. It shall make an abstract stating, in words written at length, the number of ballots cast for each office, the names of all the persons voted for, for what office, the number of votes each received, and whom they declare to be elected; which abstract shall be signed by the canvassers in their official capacity and as state canvassers, and have the seal of the state affixed. [19 G. A., ch. 163, § 14; C. '73, §§ 653, 663; R., §§ 523, 540; C. '51, §§ 289, 306.]

Sec. 1164. Record of canvass. The secretary of state shall file the abstracts when received and shall have the same bound in book form to be kept by him as a record of the result of said state election, to be known as the state election book. [32 G. A., ch. 52; C. '73, § 654; R., § 524; C. '51, § 290.]

Sec. 1165. Certificate of election. Each person declared elected by the state board of canvassers shall receive a certificate thereof, signed by the governor, or, in his absence, by the secretary of state, with the seal of state affixed, attested by the other canvassers, to be in substance as follows:

STATE OF IOWA:

To A................B................, Greeting: It is hereby certified that, at an election holden on the............day of............................, you were elected to the office of................of said state, for the term of....................years, from and after the............day of............................ (or if to fill a vacancy, for the residue of the term, ending on the............day of............................). Given at the seat of government this............day of............................

If the governor be absent, the certificate of the election of the secretary of state shall be signed by the auditor. The certificate to members of the legislature shall describe, by the number, the district from which the member is elected. [C. '73, §§ 655, 657; R., §§ 524, 527; C. '51, §§ 290, 293.]

Sec. 1167. Certificates mailed. The secretary of state shall deliver or mail certificates of election to the persons declared elected. [C. '73, §§ 648, 656, 658; R., §§ 526, 528; C. '51, §§ 291-2.]

---

*Remaining portion of this section is now obsolete.

Sec. 1166. **Representative in congress.** The certificate of the election of a representative in congress shall be signed by the governor, with a seal of the state affixed, and be countersigned by the secretary of state. [C. '73, § 658; R., § 528; C. '51, § 291.]

Sec. 1169. **Tie vote.** If more than the requisite number of persons, including presidential electors, are found to have an equal and the highest number of votes, the election of one of them shall be determined by lot. The name of each of such candidates shall be written on separate pieces of paper, as nearly uniform in size and material as possible, and placed in a receptacle so that the names cannot be seen. In the presence of the board of canvassers, one of them shall publicly draw one of such names, and such person shall be declared elected. The result of such drawing shall be entered upon the abstract of votes and duly recorded, and a certificate of election issued to such person, as provided in this chapter. [C. '73, §§ 632, 643-4, 664; R., §§ 515, 516, 541, 547; C. '51, §§ 281-2, 307, 316.]

Sec. 679. **Tie vote, city or town office.** In the event of a tie vote for any city or town office, the election shall be determined as provided in the chapter on elections.

Sec. 1170. **Canvass public—result determined.** All canvasses of returns shall be public, and the persons having the greatest number of votes shall be declared elected. [C. '73, §§ 623, 638, 664; R., §§ 497, 508, 541; C. '51, §§ 262, 273, 307.]

Sec. 1171. **Special elections—canvass and certificate.** In case a special election has been held, the board of county canvassers shall meet at one o'clock in the afternoon of the second day thereafter, and canvass the votes cast thereat. The county auditor, as soon as the canvass is completed, shall transmit to the secretary of state an abstract of the votes so canvassed, and the state board, within five days after receiving such abstracts, shall canvass the returns. A certificate of election shall be issued by the county or state board of canvassers, as in other cases. All the provisions regulating elections, obtaining returns, and canvass of votes at general elections, except as to time, shall apply to special elections. [C. '73, §§ 791-3; R., § 673.]

Sec. 1172. **Messengers for election returns.** Messengers sent for the returns of elections shall be paid from the state or county treasury, as the case may be, ten cents a mile going and returning. [C. '73, § 3827; R., § 529; C. '51, § 296.]

DIVISION XIII.

VOTING MACHINES.

Section 1137-a7. Use of voting machines authorized. That at all state, county, city, town, primary and township elections hereafter held in the state of Iowa, ballots or votes may be cast, registered, recorded, and counted by means of voting machines, as hereinafter provided. [33 G. A., ch. 72, § 1; 28 G. A., ch. 37, §1.]

Sec. 1137-a8. Board of supervisors to purchase. Hereafter the board of county supervisors of any county, or the council of any incorporated city or town in the state of Iowa may, by a two-thirds vote, authorize, purchase, and order the use of voting machines in any one or more voting precincts within said county, city, or town, until otherwise ordered by said board of county supervisors or city or town council. [28 G. A., ch. 37, § 2.]

Sec. 1137-a14. Bonds—certificates of indebtedness. The local authorities, on the adoption and purchase of a voting machine, may provide for the payment therefor in such manner as they may deem for the best interest of the locality, and may for that purpose issue bonds, certificates of indebtedness, or other obligations which shall be a charge on the county, city, or town. Such bonds, certificates, or other obligations may be issued with or without interest, payable at such time or times as the authorities may determine, but shall not be issued or sold at less than par. [28 G. A., ch. 37, § 8.]

Sec. 1137-a9. Commissioners — term — removal. Within thirty days after this act goes into effect, the governor shall appoint three commissioners and not more than two of whom shall be from the same political party. The said commissioners shall hold office for the term of five years, subject to removal at the pleasure of the governor. [28 G. A., ch. 37, § 3.]

Sec. 1137-a10. Examination of machine—report of commissioners—compensation. Any person or corporation owning or being interested in any voting machine may call upon the said commissioners to examine the said machine, and make report to the secretary of state upon the capacity of the said machine to register the will of voters, its accuracy and efficiency, and with respect to its mechanical perfections and imperfections. Their report shall be filed in the office of the secretary of state and shall state whether in their opinion the kind of machine so examined can be safely used by such voters at elections under the conditions prescribed in this act. If the report states that the machine can be so used, it shall be deemed approved by the commissioners, and machines of its kind may be adopted for use at elections as herein provided. Any form of voting machine not so approved cannot be used at any election. Each commissioner is entitled to one hundred fifty dollars for his compensation and expenses in making such examination and report, to be paid by the person or corporation applying for such examination. No commissioner shall have any interest whatever in any machine reported upon. Provided, that said commissioner shall not receive ·to exceed fifteen hundred dollars and reasonable expenses in any one year; and all sums collected for such examinations over and above said maximum salaries and expenses shall be turned into the state treasury. [28 G. A., ch. 37, § 4.]

Sec. 1137-a11. **Provisions as to the construction of machine approved.** A voting machine approved by the state board of voting machine commissioners must be so constructed as to provide facilities for voting for the candidates of at least seven different parties or organizations, must permit a voter to vote for any person for any office although not nominated as a candidate by any party or organization, and must permit voting in absolute secrecy. It must also be so constructed as to prevent voting for more than one person for the same office, except where the voter is lawfully entitled to vote for more than one person for that office; and it must afford him an opportunity to vote for any or all persons for that office as he is by law entitled to vote for and no more, at the same time preventing his voting for the same person twice. It may also be provided with one ballot in each party column or row containing only the words "presidential electors," preceded by the party name, and a vote for such ballot shall operate as a vote for all the candidates of such party for presidential electors. Such machine shall be so constructed as to accurately account for every vote cast upon it. [28 G. A., ch. 37, § 5.]

Sec. 1137-a12. **Experimental use.** The board of supervisors of any county, the council of any city or town, may provide for the experimental use at an election in one or more districts, of a machine which it might lawfully adopt, without a formal adoption thereof; and its use at such election shall be as valid for all purposes as if it had been lawfully adopted. [28 G. A., ch. 37, § 6.]

Sec. 1137-a13. **Duties of local authorities.** The local authorities adopting a voting machine shall, as soon as practicable thereafter, provide for each polling place one or more voting machines in complete working order, and shall thereafter keep them in repair, and shall have the custody thereof and of the furniture and equipment of the polling place when not in use at an election. If it shall be impracticable to supply each and every election district with a voting machine or voting machines at any election following such adoption, as many may be supplied as it is practicable to procure, and the same may be used in such election district or districts within the count⁻ city, or town as the officers adopting the same may direct. [28 G. A., ch. 37, § 7.]

Sec. 1137-a15. **Ballots—form.** All ballots shall be printed in black ink on clear, white material, of such size as will fit the ballot frame, and in plain, clear type as the space will reasonably permit. The party name for each political party represented on the machine shall be prefixed to the list of candidates of such party. The order of the list of candidates of the several parties or organizations shall be arranged as provided in section eleven hundred and six of the code, except that the lists may be arranged in horizontal rows or vertical columns. [28 G. A., ch. 37, § 9.]

Sec. 1137-a16. **Sample ballots.** The officers or board charged with the duty of providing ballots for any polling place shall provide therefor two sample ballots, which shall be arranged in the form of a diagram showing the entire front of the voting machine as it will appear after the official ballots are arranged for voting on election day. Such sample ballots shall be open to public inspection at such polling place during the day of election and the day next preceding election day. [28 G. A., ch. 37, § 10.]

Sec. 1137-a17. **Two sets of ballots.** Two sets of ballots shall be provided for each polling place for each election for use in the voting machine. [28 G. A., ch. 37, § 11.]

Sec. 1137-a18. **Delivery of ballots.** The ballots and stationery shall be delivered to the election board of each election district before ten o'clock in the forenoon of the day next preceding the election. [28 G. A., ch. 37, § 12.]

Sec. 1137-a19. Duties of election officers—independent ballots. The judges of election and clerks of each district shall meet at the polling place therein, at least three quarters of an hour before the time set for the opening of the polls at each election, and shall proceed to arrange within the guard rail the furniture, stationery, and voting machines for the conduct of the election. · The judges of election shall then and there have the voting machine, ballots, and stationery required to be delivered to them for such election; and, if it be an election at which registered voters only can vote, the registry of such electors required to be made and kept therefor. The judges shall thereupon cause at least two instruction cards to be posted conspicuously within the polling place. If not previously done, they shall arrange in their proper place on the voting machine, the ballots containing the names of the offices to be filled at such election, and the names of the candidates nominated therefor. If not previously done, the machine shall be so arranged as to show that no vote has been cast, and the same shall not be thereafter operated, except by electors in voting. Before the polls are open for election, each judge shall carefully examine every machine and see that no vote has been cast, and the same shall be subject to inspection of the election officers. Ballots voted for any person, whose name does not appear on the machine as a nominated candidate for office, are herein referred to as independent ballots. When two or more persons are to be elected to the same office, and the machine requires that all independent ballots voted for that office be deposited in a single receptacle or device, an elector may vote in or by such receptacle or device for one or more persons whose names do not appear upon the machine with or without the names of one or more persons whose names do so appear. With that exception, and except for presidential electors, no independent ballot shall be voted for any person for any office whose name appears on the machine as a nominated candidate for that office; any independent ballot so voted shall not be counted. An independent ballot must be cast in its appropriate place on the machine, or it shall be void and not counted. [28 G. A., ch. 37, § 13.]

Sec. 1137-a20. Voting machine in plain view—guard rail.

The exterior of the voting machine and every part of the polling place shall be in plain view of the election officers. The voting machine shall be placed at least three feet from every wall and partition of the polling place, and at least three feet from the guard rail, and at least four feet from the clerk's table. A guard rail shall be constructed at least three feet from the machine, with openings to admit electors to and from the machine. [28 G. A., ch. 37, § 14.]

Sec. 1137-a21. Method of voting. After the opening of the polls, the judges shall not allow any voter to pass within the guard rail until they ascertain that he is duly entitled to vote. Only one voter at a time shall be permitted to pass within the guard rail to vote. The operating of the voting machine by the elector while voting shall be secret and obscured from all other persons except as provided by this chapter in cases of voting by assisted electors. No voter shall remain within the voting machine booth longer than one minute, and if he shall refuse to leave it after the lapse of one minute, he shall be removed by the judges. [28 G. A., ch. 37, § 15.]

Sec. 1137-a22. Additional instructions. In case any elector after entering the voting machine booth shall ask for further instructions concerning the manner of voting, two judges of opposite political parties shall give such instructions to him; but no judge or other election officer or person assisting an elector shall in any manner request, suggest, or seek to persuade or induce any such elector to vote any particular ticket, or for any particular candidate, or for or against any particular amendment, question, or proposition. After receiving such instructions, such elector shall vote as in the case of an unassisted voter. [28 G. A., ch. 37, § 16.]

Sec. 1137-a23. Injury to the machine. No voter, or other person, shall deface or injure the voting machine or the ballot thereon. It shall be the duty of the judges to enforce the provisions of this section. During the entire period of an election, at least one of their number, designated by them from time to time, shall be stationed beside the entrance to the booth and shall see that it is properly closed after a voter has entered it to vote. He shall also, at such intervals as he may deem proper or necessary, examine the face of the machine to ascertain whether it has been defaced, or injured, to detect the wrongdoer and to repair any injury. [28 G. A., ch. 37, § 17.]

Sec. 1137-a24. **Canvass of vote.** As soon as the polls of the election are closed, the judges of the election thereat shall immediately lock the voting machine against voting and open the counting compartments in the presence of all persons who may be lawfully within the polling place, and proceed to canvass the vote. [28 G. A., ch. 37, § 18.]

Sec. 1137-a25. **Judges to lock machine.** The judges of election shall, as soon as the count is completed and fully ascertained as in this act required, lock the machine against voting, and it shall so remain for the period of thirty days. Whenever independent ballots have been voted, the judges shall return all of such ballots properly secured in a sealed package as prescribed by section eleven hundred forty-two of the code. [28 G. A., ch. 37, § 19.]

Sec. 1137-a26. **Written statements of election.** After the total vote for each candidate has been ascertained, and before leaving the room or voting place, the judges shall make and sign written statements of election, as required by the election laws now in force, except that such statements of the canvass need not contain any ballots except the independent ballots as herein provided. [28 G. A., ch. 37, § 20.]

Sec. 1137-a27. **What statutes apply—separate ballots.** All of the provisions of the election law now in force and not inconsistent with the provisions of this act shall apply with full force to all counties, cities, and towns adopting the use of voting machines. Nothing in this act shall be construed as prohibiting the use of a separate ballot for constitutional amendments and other public measures. [28 G. A., ch. 37, § 21.]

DIVISION XIV.

ABSENT VOTERS' LAW.

Section 1137-b. **Voters absent from county may vote.** Any qualified elector of the state of Iowa, having duly registered where such registration is required, who through the nature of his business, is absent or expects in the course of said business, to be absent from the county in which he is a qualified elector on the day of holding any general, special, primary, county, city or town election, or any qualified elector of the state of Iowa, having duly registered where such registration is required, who through illness or injury resulting in physical disability is prevented from voting in person on the day of holding any such election, may vote at any such election as hereinafter provided.   [37 G. A., ch. 419, § 3; 36 G. A., ch. 157, § 1.]

Sec. 1137-c.   **Application for official ballot.**   Any elector, as defined in the foregoing section, expecting to be absent from the county of his residence on the day of any such election or any elector physically unable to go to the polls on the day of such election may, not more than fifteen nor less than three days prior to the date of such election, make application to the county auditor of such county, or the clerk of the city or town, as the case may be, for an official ballot to be voted at such election.   [37 G. A., ch. 419, § 4; 36 G. A., ch. 157, § 2.]

Sec. 1137-d.   **Form of application.**   Application for such ballot shall be made on a blank to be furnished by the county auditor or clerk of the city or town, as the case may be, in which the applicant is an elector, and shall be substantially in the following form:

APPLICATION FOR BALLOT TO BE VOTED AT THE..............................
ELECTION ON...
State of...............................⎫ ss.
County of...............................⎭
  I, ..., do solemnly swear that I have been a resident of the state of Iowa for six months, of the county of...for sixty days and of the ....precinct of...................................ward of the city or town of...................................ten days next preceding this election, and that I am a duly qualified elector entitled to vote at said election. That I am...and because
                                   (Stating business)
of the nature of my business expect to be absent from said county on ...., the date of said election, or because of physical inability to attend the polls, and I hereby make application for an official ballot or ballots to be voted by me at such election, and that I will return said ballot or ballots to the officer issuing same, on or before the day of said election.
Date...
                                   Signed...
Residence, (street and number)...
  (City)...............................P. O. Address...
  Subscribed and sworn to before me this...
day of..., A. D. 191.........

....
                    (Penalty clause set out in full.)

Provided that if the application be made for a primary election ballot, such application shall designate the name of the political party with which the applicant is affiliated. [37 G. A., ch. 419, § 5; 36 G. A., ch. 157, § 3.]

Sec. 1137-e. **Auditor or clerk to deliver or mail ballot.** Upon receipt of such application and not more than ten nor less than three days prior to such election, it shall be the duty of such auditor or clerk, as the case may be, to mail, postage prepaid, an official ballot or ballots, if more than one are to be voted at said election, or such officer shall deliver said ballot or ballots to any qualified elector applying in person at the office of such auditor or clerk, as the case may be, and subscribing to the foregoing application, not more than ten nor less than one secular day before said election. [36 G. A., ch. 157, § 4.]

Sec. 1137-f. **Duty of auditor—form of affidavit.** It shall be the duty of said auditor or clerk, as the case may be, to fold the ballot or ballots in the manner specified in section eleven hundred sixteen of the code and he shall inclose such ballot or ballots in an envelope unsealed to be furnished by him, which envelope shall bear upon the face thereof the name, official title and postoffice address of such auditor or clerk, and upon the other side a printed affidavit in substantially the following form:

State of................................⎱ ss.
County of..............................⎰

I, ..., do solemnly swear that the following matters stated in this affidavit relating to my qualifications for registration and voting are true; residence number......................
....street, city, village or township of
...., ...county, Iowa.
Age.....................years. Nativity.............................. Color......................
Term of residence in precinct..
Term of residence in county..
Term of residence in state..
Naturalized.................................... Date of naturalization papers.....................
Court in which naturalized..; whether by act of congress............................ Whether qualified voter...........................;
date of application............................ Last preceding place of-residence.., number....................................
street, city, village or township, ...,
county, Iowa. That I am engaged in the business or work of........................
....; that I will be absent from the county of my residence or that my physical condition is such to prevent my attending the

polls on the day of election, and that I have marked the enclosed ballot in secret.

Signed...

Subscribed and sworn to before me this..day of
...., A. D. ...., and I hereby certify .
that the affiant exhibited the enclosed ballot to me unmarked; that he then in my presence and in the presence of no other person, and in such manner that I could not see his vote, marked such ballot and inclosed and sealed the same in this envelope; that the affiant was not solicited or advised by me for or against any candidate or measure.

....

....

Provided that if the ballot inclosed is to be voted at a primary election, the affidavit shall designate the name of the political party with which the voter is affiliated. [37 G. A., ch. 419, § 1; 36 G. A., ch. 157, § 5.]

Sec. 1137-g. Affidavit—marking ballot—ballot deposited in envelope—mailing or delivering envelope. Such absent or disabled voter shall make and subscribe to the said affidavit before an officer authorized by law to administer oaths and such voter shall thereupon in the presence of such officer and of no other person, mark such ballot or ballots, but in such manner that such officer cannot know how such ballot is marked, and such ballot or ballots shall then in the presence of such officer be folded by such voter so that each ballot will be separate and so as to conceal the marking and be in the presence of such officer deposited in such envelope and the envelope securely sealed. Said envelope shall be mailed by such voter, by registered mail, postage prepaid, to the officer issuing the ballot, or if more convenient it may be delivered in person. [37 G. A., ch. 419, § 6; 36 G. A., ch. 157, § 6.]

Sec. 1137-h. Custody of ballot by auditor or clerk. Upon receipt of such absent voter's ballot, the auditor or clerk, as the case may be, shall forthwith inclose the same, unopened, together with the application made by said absent voter, in a larger or carrier envelope which shall be securely sealed and indorsed with the name and official title of such auditor or clerk, and the words, "this envelope contains an absent voter's ballot, or disabled voter's ballot, (as the case may be) and must be opened only at the polls on election day while said polls are open," and such auditor or clerk shall thereafter safely keep the same in his office until delivered by him as provided in the next section. [37 G. A., ch. 419, § 7; 36 G. A., ch. 157, § 7.]

Sec. 1137-i. **Envelopes—delivery to judges of election.** In case an absent or disabled voter's ballot is received by the auditor or clerk, as the case may be, prior to the delivery of the official ballots to the judges of election of the precinct in which said elector resides, such ballot envelope and application, sealed in the carrier envelope, shall be inclosed in such package and therewith delivered to the judges of such precinct. In case the official ballots for such precinct have been delivered to the judges of election at the time of the receipt by the auditor or clerk of such absent or disabled voter's ballot, such official shall immediately inclose said envelope containing the absent or disabled voter's ballot, together with his application therefor, in a larger or carrier envelope which shall be securely sealed and indorsed on the face to the judges of election, giving the name or number of precinct, street and number of the polling place, city or town in which such absent or disabled voter is a qualified elector and the words "this envelope contains an absent voter's ballot, or disabled voter's ballot, (as the case may be) and must be opened only on election day at the polls while the polls are open", mailing the same, postage prepaid, to such judges of election or, if more convenient, such auditor or clerk may deliver such absent or disabled voter's ballot to the judges of election in person or by duly deputized agent, said auditor, clerk or agent to secure his receipt for delivery of such ballot or ballots. Provided, however, that such delivery of ballots by person is to be made without expense to the county, city or town, as the case may be. [37 G. A., ch. 419, § 8; 36 G. A., ch. 157, § 8.]

Sec. 1137-j. **Opening envelope—depositing ballot—rejecting ballot.** At any time between the opening and closing of the polls on such election day the judges of election of said precinct shall open the outer or carrier envelope only, announce the absent or disabled voter's name and compare the signature upon the application with the signature upon the affidavit on the ballot envelope. In case the judges find the affidavits executed; that the signatures correspond; the applicant a duly qualified elector of the precinct and that the applicant has not voted in person at said election, they shall open the envelope containing the absent or disabled voter's ballot in such manner as not to deface or destroy the affidavit thereon and take out the ballot or ballots therein contained without unfolding or permitting the same to be unfolded or examined and having indorsed the ballot in like manner as other ballots are required to be indorsed, deposit the same in the proper ballot box or boxes and enter the absent or disabled voter's name in the poll book, the same as if he had been present and voted in person. In case such affidavit is found to be insufficient, or that the signatures do not correspond, or that the applicant is not a duly qualified elector in such precinct, or that the ballot envelope is open, or has been opened and resealed, or that the ballot envelope contains more than one ballot of any one kind, such vote shall not be accepted or counted. Every ballot not counted shall be indorsed on the back thereof "rejected (giving reason therefor)". All rejected ballots shall be inclosed and securely sealed in an envelope on which the judges shall indorse "defective ballots" with a statement of the precinct in which and the date of the election at which they were cast, signed by the judges and returned to the same officer and in the same manner as by law provided for the return and preservation of official ballots voted at such election.

The affidavit upon the ballot envelope shall constitute a sufficient registration of the voter in precincts where registration is required and shall be treated like and have the same force and effect as a certificate issued by the registers of election on election day in all cases where the voter is not already registered and where his name does not appear upon the alphabetical lists, and if the ballot be deposited and the absent or disabled voter's name be entered on the poll books as herein provided, the judges of election shall enter the absent or disabled voter's name on the alphabetical lists with the same data as is entered when a certificate of registration is filed and the ballot envelope having the absent or disabled voter's affidavit thereon· shall be preserved and returned with the certificates of registration, poll book and alphabetical lists to the city clerk who shall preserve the same, and it shall be used by the registers of election, in precincts where registration is required in making up the new registry lists from the poll books, and such affidavit shall serve as the registration record of the voter for the new registry books and lists. If the ballot is rejected and the vote of the absent or disabled voter not accepted or counted as provided herein said ballot envelope with the affidavit of the absent or disabled voter indorsed thereon shall be returned with said rejected ballot in the envelope indorsed "defective ballots". [37 G. A., ch. 419, § 2; 36 G. A., ch. 157, § 9.]

Sec. 1137-k. Challenges. The vote of any absent or disabled voter may be challenged for cause and the judges of election shall have all the power and authority given by law to hear and determine the legality of such ballot. [37 G. A., ch. 419, § 9; 36 G. A., ch. 157, § 10.]

Sec. 1137-l. Ballot of deceased voter. Whenever it shall be made to appear by due proof to the judges of election that any elector, who has marked and forwarded his ballot as provided in this act, has died, then the ballot of such deceased voter shall be returned by the judges of election with the unused ballots to the official issuing it, however the casting of the ballot of a deceased voter shall not invalidate the election. [36 G. A., ch. 157, § 11.]

Sec. 1137-m. Laws made applicable. All the provisions of the election laws now in force and not inconsistent with the provisions of this act, shall apply with full force and effect to all counties, cities and towns in which voting machines are used, relative to the furnishing of ballot boxes; the printing and furnishing of official ballots in such number as the auditor or clerk, as the case may be, may deem necessary; the canvassing of the ballots and making the proper return of the result of the election. [36 G. A., ch. 157, § 12.]

Sec. 1137-n. Penalty clause. If any person shall wilfully swear falsely to any such affidavit, he shall, upon conviction thereof, be guilty of perjury and shall be punished as in such cases by law provided. If any person who, having procured an official ballot or ballots as heretofore provided, shall wilfully neglect or refuse to cast or return same in the manner heretofore provided, or shall wilfully violate any provision of this act, he shall be guilty of a misdemeanor and shall be fined not to exceed one hundred dollars, or imprisoned in the county jail not to exceed thirty days. If any county auditor, city or town clerk or any election officer, shall refuse or neglect to perform any of the duties prescribed by this act, or shall violate any of the provisions thereof, he shall upon conviction be fined not less than one hundred dollars nor more than one thousand dollars, or imprisoned in the county jail not to exceed ninety days. [36 G. A., ch. 157, § 13.]

Sec. 1137-o. Construction of statute. This act shall be deemed to provide a method of voting in addition to the method now provided by statute, and, to such extent, as amendatory of existing statutes relating to the manner and method of voting. [36 G. A., ch. 157, § 14.]

DIVISION XV.

PRESIDENTIAL ELECTORS.

Section 1173. Election—canvass—women entitled to vote. At the general election in the years of the presidential election, or at such other times as the congress of the United States may direct, there shall be elected by the electors of the state, one person from each congressional district into which the state is divided, as elector of president and vice president, and two from the state at large, no one of whom shall be a person holding the office of senator or representative in congress, or any office of trust or profit under the United States. Each elector of each congressional district and each elector at large nominated by any party or group of petitioners shall receive the combined vote of the electors of the state for the candidates for president and vice president of such party or group of[1] petitioners, and a vote cast for the candidates for president and vice president of the United States shall be the votes of the voter for the electors of the respective party or group of petitioners. The canvass of the votes for candidates for president and vice president of the United States and the returns thereof shall be a canvass and return of the votes cast for the electors of the same party or group of petitioners respectively, and the certificate of such election made by the governor shall be in accord with such return. Provided, however, that the right to vote for presidential electors shall not be denied or abridged on account of sex, and that every woman who has attained the age of twenty-one (21) years and who possesses all other qualifications requisite to a male voter, shall be entitled to vote, the same as men, at any election held for the purpose of electing presidential electors. [38 G. A., ch. 353, § 1; 38 G. A., ch. 86, § 6; 28 G. A., ch. 38, § 1; 16 G. A., ch. 23; C. '73, §§ 659, 660; R., §§ 535-6; C. '51, §§ 301-2.]

---

[1]"or" in enrolled bill.

Sec. 1168. Certificate to electors. The governor, at the expiration of ten days from the completed canvass, shall issue to each presidential elector declared elected a certificate of his election, under his hand and the seal of state, the same, in substance, as required in other cases, and shall notify him to attend at the seat of government at noon on the second Monday in January following his election, reporting his attendance to him. If there be a contest of the election, no certificate shall issue until it is determined. [22 G. A., ch. 50; C. '73, § 665; R., § 542; C. '51, § 308.]

Sec. 1174. Meeting—certificate. The presidential electors shall meet in the capitol, at the seat of government, at noon of the second Monday in January after their election, or s soon thereafter as practicable. If, at the time of such meeting any elector for any cause is absent, those present shall at once proceed to elect, from the citizens of the state, a substitute elector or electors, and certify the choice so made to the governor, and he shall immediately cause the person or persons so selected to be notified thereof. [22 G. A., ch. 50; C. '73, §§ 665-7; R., §§ 542-4; C. '51, §§ 308-10.]

Sec. 1175. Certificate of governor. When so met, the said electors shall proceed, in the manner pointed out by law, with the election and the governor shall duly certify the result thereof, under the seal of the state, to the United States secretary of state, and as required by act of congress relating to such elections. [22 G. A., ch. 50; C. '73, § 668; R., § 545; C. '51, § 311.]

Sec. 1176. Compensation. The electors shall each receive a compensation of five dollars for every day's attendance, and the same mileage as members of the general assembly. [C. '73, § 669; R., § 546; C. '51, § 312.]

DIVISION XVI.
STATEMENT OF EXPENSES.

Section 1137-a1. Candidates to make sworn statement of election expenses—where filed. Every candidate for any office to be voted for at any primary, municipal or general election shall, within ten days after the holding of such primary, municipal or general election, file a true, correct, detailed, sworn statement showing each and all sums of money or other things of value disbursed, expended or promised directly or indirectly by him, and to the best of his knowledge and belief by any other person or persons in his behalf for the purpose of aiding or securing his nomination or election. If the person be a candidate for a municipal or a county office, such statement shall be filed with the county auditor; if for a state office, or any other office to be voted for by the electors of more than one county, such statement shall be filed with the secretary of state. Such statement shall show the dates, amounts, and from whom such sums of money or other things of value were received, and the dates, amounts, purposes and to whom paid or disbursed, and shall include the assessment of any person, committee, or organization in charge of the campaign of such candidate. [32 G. A., ch. 50, § 2.]

Sec. 1137-a2. Testimony—immunity from prosecution. In prosecutions under this act, no witness shall be excused from giving testimony on the ground that his testimony would tend to render him criminally liable or expose him to public ignominy, but any matter so elicited shall not be used against him, and said witness shall not be prosecuted for any crime connected with or growing out of the act on which the prosecution is based in the cause in which his evidence is used for the state, under the provisions of this section. [32 G. A., ch. 50, § 3.]

Sec. 1137-a3. Statements by committee chairman. The chairman of each party central committee for the state, district or county, shall file a statement of receipts and expenditures within ten days after the general election. The chairman of state and district central committees shall file said statements with the secretary of state; and the chairman of county central committees, with the county auditor. Such statements shall contain all the information required to be filed by candidates as set forth in section two of this act, and in addition thereto shall state the amounts or balances remaining on hand. The person filing the same shall make oath that it is a full, true and correct statement. [32 G. A., ch. 50, § 4.]

Sec. 1137-a4. Statements open to public inspection. The statements provided for in this act shall be open at all times to the inspection of the public, and remain on file and become a part of the permanent records in the office where filed. [32 G. A., ch. 50, § 5.]

Sec. 1137-a5. **Treating near the polls—duty of judges and clerks.** It shall be the duty of the judges and clerks of all municipal, general and primary elections to prohibit the placing, keeping, and giving to the voters by any person of any cigars, food or other refreshments or treats, in or about the polling place. [32 G. A., ch. 50, § 6.]

Sec. 1137-a6. **Penalty.** Any person violating any of the provisions of the last five preceding sections shall be deemed guilty of a misdemeanor, and upon conviction thereof shall be punished by a fine of not less than fifty dollars nor more than three hundred dollars, or by imprisonment in the county jail not less than thirty days nor more than six months. [32 G. A., ch. 50, § 7.]

DIVISION XVII.

CONTESTING ELECTIONS: GENERAL PROVISIONS.

Section 1198. **Grounds of contest.** The election of any person to any county office, or to a seat in either branch of the general assembly, may be contested by any person eligible to such office; and the election of any person to a state office, or to the office of presidential elector, by any eligible person who received votes for the same office, and the grounds therefor shall be as follows:

1. Misconduct, fraud or corruption on the part of judges of election in any precinct, or of any board of canvassers, or any member of either board, sufficient to change the result.

2. That the incumbent was not eligible to the office at the time of election.

3. That the incumbent has been duly convicted of an infamous crime before the election, and the judgment has not been reversed, annulled or set aside, nor the incumbent pardoned, at the time of election.

4. That the incumbent has given or offered to any elector, or any judge, clerk or canvasser of the election, any bribe or reward in money, property or thing of value, for the purpose of procuring his election.

5. That illegal votes have been received or legal votes rejected at the polls, sufficient to change the result.

8

6. Any error in any board of canvassers in counting the votes, or in declaring the result of the election, if the error would affect the result.

7. Any other cause which shows that another person was the person duly elected. [22 G. A., ch. 49, §1; C. '73, §§ 692, 718, 730, 737; R., §§ 569, 571, 598, 610, 617; C. '51, §§ 339, 341, 368, 380, 387.]

Sec. 1219. Certificate withheld. If notice of contesting the election of an officer is filed before the certificate of election is delivered to him, it shall be withheld until the determination of the contest. [C. '73, § 713; R., § 597; C. '51, § 367.]

Sec. 1199. Incumbent. The term "incumbent" in this chapter means the person whom the canvassers declare elected. [C. '73, § 693; R., § 570; C. '51, § 340.]

Sec. 1200. Change the result. When the misconduct, fraud or corruption complained of is on the part of the judges of election in a precinct, it shall not be held sufficient to set aside the election, unless the rejection of the vote of that precinct would change the result as to that office. [C. '73, § 694; R., § 572; C. '51, § 342.]

Sec. 1143. Recanvass in case of contest. The parties to any contested election shall have the right, in open session of the court or tribunal trying the contest, and in the presence of the officer having them in custody, to have the ballots opened, and all errors of the judges in counting or refusing to count ballots corrected by such court or tribunal. [33 G. A., ch. 73, § 1; 24 G. A., ch. 33, § 25.]

Sec. 1250. Provisions applicable. All the provisions of this chapter in relation to contested elections of county officers shall be applicable, as near as may be, to contested elections for other offices, except as herein otherwise provided, and in all cases process and papers may be issued to and served by the sheriff of any county. [22 G. A., ch. 49, § 6; C. '73, §§ 729, 745; R., §§ 609, 626; C. '51, §§ 379, 396.]

DIVISION XVIII.
CONTESTING ELECTIONS OF GOVERNOR AND LIEU-TENANT GOVERNOR.

Section 1239. Contest as to governor and lieutenant governor. The contestant for the office of governor or lieutenant governor shall, within thirty days after the proclamation of the result of the election, deliver to the presiding officer of each house of the general assembly a notice of his intent to contest, and a specification of the grounds of such contest, as before directed. [C. '73, § 738; R., § 618; C. '51, § 388.]
See Const., Art. IV, § 5.

Sec. 1240. Notice to incumbent. As soon as the presiding officers have received the notice and specifications, they shall make out a notice, directed to the incumbent, including a copy of the specifications, which shall be served by the sergeant-at-arms. [C. '73, § 739; R., § 619; C. '51, § 389.]

Sec. 1241. Houses notified. The presiding officers shall also immediately make known to their respective houses that such notice and specifications have been received. [C. '73, § 740; R., § 620; C. '51, § 390.]

Sec. 1242. Court—how chosen. Each house shall forthwith proceed, separately, to choose seven members of its own body in the following manner:

1. The names of members of each house, except the presiding officer, written on similar paper tickets, shall be placed in a box, the names of the senators in their presence by their secretary, and the names of the representatives in their presence by their clerk.

2. The secretary of the senate in the presence of the senate, and the clerk of the house of representatives in the presence of the house, shall draw from their respective boxes the names of seven members each.

3. As soon as the names are thus drawn, the names of the members drawn by each house shall be communicated to the other, and entered on the journals of each house. [C. '73, § 741; R., § 621; C. '51, § 391.]

Sec. 1243. Powers and proceedings of committee. The members thus drawn shall constitute a committee to try and determine the contested election, and for that purpose shall hold their meetings publicly at the place where the general assembly is sitting, at such times as they may designate; and may adjourn from day to day or to a day certain, not more than four days distant, until such trial is determined; shall have power to send for persons and papers, and to take all necessary means to procure testimony, extending like privileges to the contestant and the incumbent; and shall report their judgment to both branches of the general assembly, which report shall be entered on the journals of both houses. [C. '73, § 742; R., § 622; C. '51, § 392.]

Sec. 1244. Testimony. The testimony shall be confined to the matters contained in the specifications. [C. '73, § 743; R., § 623; C. '51, § 393.]

Sec. 1245. Judgment. The judgment of the committee pronounced in the final decision on the election shall be conclusive. [C. '73, § 744; R., § 624; C. '51, § 394.]

DIVISION XIX.

CONTESTING ELECTIONS FOR SEATS IN GENERAL ASSEMBLY.

Section 1233. Contest as to member of general assembly. The contestant for a seat in either branch of the general assembly shall, within thirty days after the incumbent was declared elected, serve on the incumbent a statement as required in relation to county officers, except the list of illegal votes, which shall be served with the notice of taking depositions relative to them, and if no such deposition is taken, then twenty days before the first day of the next session. [C. '73, § 731; R., § 611; C. '51, §381.]

Sec. 1234. Subpoenas. Any judge or clerk of a court of record may issue subpoenas in the above cases, as in those before provided, and compel the attendance of witnesses thereunder. [C. '73, § 732; R., § 612; C. '51, § 382.]

Sec. 1235. Depositions. Depositions may be taken in such cases in the same manner and under the same rules as in an action at law in the district court, but no cause for taking the same need be shown. [C. '73, § 733; R., § 613; C. '51, § 383.]

Sec. 1236. Return of depositions. A copy of the statement, and of the notice for taking depositions, with the service indorsed, and verified by affidavit if not served by an officer, shall be returned to the officer taking the depositions, and then, with the depositions, shall be sealed up and transmitted to the secretary of state, with an indorsement thereon showing the nature of the papers, the names of the contesting parties, and the branch of the general assembly before whom the contest is to be tried. [C. '73, § 734; R., § 614; C. '51, § 384.]

Sec. 1237. **Statement and depositions—notice.** The secretary shall deliver the same unopened to the presiding officer of the house in which the contest is to be tried, on or before the second day of the session, regular or special, of the general assembly next after taking the depositions, and the presiding officer shall immediately give notice to his house that such papers are in his possession. [C. '73, § 735; R., § 615; C. '51, § 385.]

Sec. 1238. **Power of general assembly.** Nothing herein contained shall be construed to abridge the right of either branch of the general assembly to grant commissions to take depositions, or to send for and examine any witness it may desire to hear on such trial. [C. '73, § 736; R., § 616; C. '51, § 386.]

DIVISION XX.

CONTESTING ELECTIONS OF PRESIDENTIAL ELECTOR.

Section 1246. **Contest as to presidential electors.** The court for the trial of contested elections for presidential electors shall consist of the chief justice of the supreme court, who shall be presiding judge of the court, and four judges of the district court not interested, to be selected by the supreme court, two of whom, with the chief justice, shall constitute a quorum for the transaction of the business of the court. If the chief justice should for any cause be unable to attend at the trial, the judge longest on the supreme court bench shall preside in place of the chief justice; and any question arising as to the membership of the court shall be determined by the members of the court not interested in the question. The secretary of state shall be the clerk of the court, or, in his absence or inability to act, the clerk of the supreme court. Each member of the court, before entering upon the discharge of his duties, shall take an oath before the secretary of state, or some officer qualified to administer oaths, that he will support the constitution of the United States and that of the state of Iowa, and that, without fear, favor, affection, or hope of reward, he will, to the best of his knowledge and ability, administer justice according to law and the facts in the case. [22 G. A., ch. 49, § 2.]

Sec. 1247. Statement. The contestant shall file the statement provided for in this chapter in the office of the secretary of the state, within ten days from the day on which the returns are canvassed by the state board of canvassers, and, within the same time, serve a copy of the same, with a notice of the contest, on the incumbent. [22 G. A., ch. 49, § 3.]

Sec. 1248. Trial. The clerk of the court shall, immediately after the filing of the statement, notify the judges herein named, and fix a day for the organization of the court within three days thereafter, and also notify the parties to the contest. The judges shall meet on the day fixed, and organize the court, and make and announce such rules for the trial of the case as they shall think necessary for the protection of the rights of each party and a just and speedy trial of the case, and commence the trial of the case as early as practicable thereafter, and so arrange for and conduct the trial that a final determination of the same and judgment shall be rendered at least six days before the second Monday in January next following. [22 G. A., ch. 49, § 4.]

Sec. 1249. Judgment. The judgment of the court shall determine which of the parties to the action is entitled to hold the office of presidential elector, and shall be authenticated by the presiding judge and clerk of the court and filed with the secretary of state; and the judgment so rendered shall constitute a final determination of the title to the office, and a certificate of appointment shall be issued to the successful party as an elector. [22 G. A., ch. 49, § 5.]

DIVISION XXI.

CONTESTING ELECTIONS OF STATE OFFICERS.

Section 1224. State court of contest. The court for the trial of contested state elections, except of governor and lieutenant governor, shall consist of three judges, not interested, of the supreme court or district court, or any of them, as may be convenient. [C. '73, § 719; R., § 599; C. '51, § 369.]

Sec. 1225. **Clerk.** The secretary of state shall be the clerk of this court; but if the person holding that office is a party to the contest, the clerk of the supreme court, or, in case of his absence or inability, the auditor of state, shall be clerk. [C. '73, §720; R., § 600; C. '51, § 370.]

Sec. 1226. **Statement** filed. The statement must be filed with such clerk within thirty days from the day when incumbent was declared elected. [C. '73, § 721; R., § 601; C. '51, § 371.]

Sec. 1227. **Time of trial—notice.** The clerk shall, as soon as practicable, ascertain which three of the judges residing nearest the seat of government can attend the trial, fix a time therefor, and notify the judges, and cause a copy of the statement and a notice of the time fixed for trial to be served upon the incumbent, and a notice of the time to be served upon the contestant, at least twenty days before the day of trial, and returns thereof to be made to him; when convenient, the service of the above papers may be made by the clerk of this court. The time for the trial shall not be set beyond the last Monday of January following the election. [C. '73, § 722; R., § 601; C. '51, §§ 371-2.]

Sec. 1229. **Place of trial.** The trial shall take place at the seat of government, unless some other place be substituted by consent of the court and both parties. [C. '73, § 725; R., § 605; C. '51, § 375.]

Sec. 1228. **Subpoenas—depositions.** The secretary of state, the several clerks of the supreme and district courts, under their respective seals of office, and either of the judges of the supreme or district courts, under their hands, may issue subpoenas for witnesses to attend this court; and disobedience to such process may be treated as a contempt. Depositions may also be taken as in the case of contested county elections. [C. '73, § 723; R., § 603; C. '51, § 373.]

Sec. 1231. **Judgment filed—execution.** A transcript of the judgment rendered by such court, filed in the office of the clerk of the supreme court, shall have the force and effect of a judgment of the supreme court, and execution may issue therefrom in the first instance against the party's property generally. [C. '73, § 727; R., § 607; C. '51, § 377.]

Sec. 1232. **Power of judge.** The presiding judge of this court shall have authority to carry into effect any order of the court, after the adjournment thereof, by attachment or otherwise. [C. '73, § 728; R., § 608; C. '51, § 378.]

Sec. 1230. **Compensation of judges.** The judges shall be entitled to receive for their travel and attendance the sum of six dollars each per day, with such mileage as is allowed to members of the general assembly, to be paid from the state treasury. [C. '73, § 726; R., § 606; C. '51, § 376.]

DIVISION XXII.
CONTESTING ELECTIONS OF COUNTY OFFICERS.

Section 1201. **Court—how constituted.** The court for the trial of contested county elections shall be thus constituted: The chairman of the board of supervisors shall be the presiding officer, and the contestant and incumbent may each name a person who shall be associated with him. [C. '73, § 695; R., 573; C. '51, § 343.]

Sec. 1206. **Judges.** The contestant and incumbent shall each file in the auditor's office, on or before the day of trial, a written nomination of one associate judge of the contested election, who shall be sworn in manner and form as trial jurors are in trials of civil actions; if either the contestant or the incumbent fails to nominate, the presiding judge shall appoint for him. When either of the nominated judges fails to appear on the day of trial, his place may be filled by another appointment under the same rule. [C. '73, § 700; R., §§ 577-8; C. '51, §§ 347-8.]

Sec. 1202. **Clerk.** The county auditor shall be clerk of this court, and keep all papers, and record the proceedings in the election book, in manner similar to the record of the proceedings of the district court, but when the county auditor is a party, the court shall appoint a suitable person as clerk, whose appointment shall be recorded. [C. '73, § 696; R., § 571; C. '51, § 344.]

Sec. 1214. **Sheriff to attend.** The court or presiding judge may direct the attendance of the sheriff or a constable when necessary. [C. '73, § 708; R., § 589; C. '51, § 359.]

Sec. 1203. **Statement of contest.** The contestant shall file in the office of the county auditor, within twenty days after the day when the incumbent was declared elected, a written statement of his intention to contest the election, setting forth the name of the contestant, and that he or she is qualified to hold such office, the name of the incumbent, the office contested, the time of the election, and the particular causes of contest, which statement shall be verified by the affidavit of the contestant, or some elector of the county, that the causes set forth are true as he verily believes. The contestant must also file with the county auditor a bond, with security to be approved by said auditor, conditioned to pay all costs in case the election be confirmed, or the statement be dismissed, or the prosecution fail. When the auditor is a party, the clerk of the district court shall receive such statement and approve such bond. [C. '73, § 697; R., § 575; C. '51, § 345.]

Sec. 1204. **Names of voters.** When the reception of illegal or the rejection of legal votes is alleged as a cause of contest, the names of the persons who so voted, or whose votes were rejected, with the precinct where they voted or offered to vote, shall be set forth in the statement. [C. '73, § 698; R., § 576; C. '51, § 346.]

Sec. 1205. **Trial—notice.** The chairman of the board of supervisors shall thereupon fix a day for the trial, not more than thirty nor less than twenty days thereafter, and shall cause a notice of such trial to be served on the incumbent, with a copy of the contestant's statement, at least ten days before the day set for trial. [C. '73, § 699; R., §§ 577, 579, 580; C. '51, §§ 347, 349, 350.]

Sec. 1213. **Place of trial.** The trial of contested county elections shall take place at the county seat, unless some other place within the county is substituted by the consent of the court and parties. [C. '73, § 703; R., § 587; C. '51, § 357.]

Sec. 1210. **Subpoenas.** Subpoenas for witnesses may be issued at any time after the notice of trial is served, either by the clerk of the district court or by the county auditor, and shall command the witnesses to appear at......................................,
on...................., to testify in relation to a contested election, wherein A..............B..............is contestant and C..............
D..............is incumbent. [C. '73, § 704; R., §§ 582, 586; C. '51, §§ 352, 356.]

Sec. 1207. **Postponement.** The trial shall proceed at the time appointed, unless postponed for good cause shown by affidavit, the terms of which postponement shall be in the discretion of the court. [C. '73, § 701; R., § 583; C. '51, § 353.]

Sec. 1208. **Procedure—powers of court.** The proceedings shall be assimilated to those in an action, so far as practicable, but shall be under the control and direction of the court, which shall have all the powers of the district court necessary to the right hearing and determination of the matter, to compel the attendance of witnesses, swear them and direct their examination, to punish for contempt in its presence or by disobedience to its lawful mandate, to adjourn from day to day, to make any order concerning intermediate costs, and to enforce its orders by attachment. It shall be governed by the rules of law and evidence applicable to the case. [C. '73, § 702; R., §§ 584, 588, 591; C. '51, §§ 354, 358, 361.]

Sec. 1211. **Sufficiency of statement—amendment.** The statement shall not be dismissed for want of form, if the particular causes of contest are alleged with such certainty as will sufficiently advise the incumbent of the real grounds of contest. If any part of the causes are held insufficient, they may be amended, but the incumbent will be entitled to an adjournment, if he states on oath that he has matter of answer to the amended causes, for the preparation of which he needs further time. Such adjournment shall be upon such terms as the court thinks reasonable; but if all the causes are held insufficient and an amendment is asked, the adjournment shall be at the cost of contestant. If no amendment is asked for or made, or in case of entire failure to prosecute, the proceedings may be dismissed. [C. '73, § 705; R., §§ 585, 591; C. '51, §§ 355, 361.]

Sec. 1209. **Testimony.** The testimony may be oral or by deposition, taken as in an action at law in the district court. [C. '73, § 703; R., § 581; C. '51, § 351.]

Sec. 1215. **Voters testify.** The court may require any person called as a witness, who voted at such election, to answer touching his qualifications as a voter, and, if he was not a qualified voter in the county where he voted, then to answer for whom he voted; and if the witness answer such questions, no part of his testimony on that trial shall be used against him in any criminal action. [C. '73, § 709; R., § 590; C. '51, § 360.]

Sec. 1220. **Judgment.** The court shall pronounce judgment whether the incumbent or any other person was duly elected, and adjudge that the person so declared elected will be entitled to his certificate. If the judgment be against the incumbent, and he has already received the certificate, the judgment shall annul it. If the court find that no person was elected, the judgment shall be that the election be set aside. [C. '73, § 714; R., § 592; C. '51, § 362.]

Sec. 1221. **How enforced.** When either the contestant or incumbent shall be in possession of the office, by holding over or otherwise, the pres·ding judge shall, if the judgment be against the party so in possession of the office and in favor of his antagonist, issue an order to carry into effect the judgment of the court, which order shall be under the seal of the county, and shall command the sheriff of the county to put the successful party into possession of the office without delay, and to deliver to him all books and papers belonging to the same; and the sheriff shall execute such order as other writs. [C. '73, § 715.]

Sec. 1222. **Appeal.** The party against whom judgment is rendered may appeal within twenty days to the district court, but, if he be in possession of the office, such appeal will not supersede the execution of the judgment of the court as provided in the preceding section, unless he gives a bond, with security to be approved by the district judge, in a sum to be fixed by him, and which shall be at least double the probable compensation of such officer for six months, which bond shall be conditioned that he will prosecute his appeal without delay, and that, if the judgment appealed from be affirmed, he will pay over to the successful party all compensation received by him while in possession of said office after the judgment appealed from was rendered. The court shall hear the appeal in equity and determine anew all questions arising in the case. [28 G. A., ch. 39, § 1; C. '73, § 716.]

Sec. 1223. **Judgment on appeal.** If, upon appeal, the judgment is affirmed, the district court may render judgment upon the bond for the amount of damages, against the appellant and the sureties thereon. [C. '73, § 717.]

Sec. 1212. **Process—fees.** The style, form and manner of service of process and papers, and the fees of officers and witnesses, shall be the same as in the district court, so far as the nature of the case admits. [C. '73, §§ 706, 724; R., §§ 586, 604; C. '51, §§ 356, 374.]

Sec. 1216. **Compensation of** judges. The judges shall be entitled to receive four dollars a day for the time occupied by the trial. [C. '73, § 710; R., § 593; C. '51, § 363.]

Sec. 1217. **Costs.** The contestant and the incumbent are liable to the officers and witnesses for the costs made by them, respectively; but if the election be confirmed, or the statement be dismissed or the prosecution fail, judgment shall be rendered against the contestant for costs; and if the judgment be against the incumbent, or the election be set aside, it shall be against him for costs. [C. '73, § 711; R., § 594; C. '51, § 364.]

Sec. 1218. **How collected.** A transcript of the judgment, filed and recorded in the office of the clerk of the district court as provided in relation to transcripts from justices' courts, shall have the same effect as there provided, and execution may issue thereon. [C. '73, § 712; R., § 595; C. '51, § 365.]

DIVISION XXIII.

CONTESTING ELECTIONS OF CITY OR TOWN OFFICERS.

Section 678. **Contesting elections.** The election of any person to a city or town office may be contested upon the same grounds and in the manner provided for contesting elections to county offices, so far as applicable. The mayor shall be one of the court and the presiding officer thereof, and, if his election is contested, the council shall select one of its members to act in his place.

DIVISION XXIV.

CONTRIBUTIONS BY CORPORATIONS PROHIBITED.

Section 1641-h. **Political contributions prohibited.** It shall be unlawful for any corporation doing business within the state, or any officer, agent or representative thereof acting for such corporation, to give or contribute any money, property, labor or thing of value, directly or indirectly, to any member of any political committee, political party, or employe or representative thereof, or to any candidate for any public office or candidate for nomination to any public office or to the representative of such candidate, for campaign expenses or for any political purpose whatsoever, or to any person, partnership or corporation for the purpose of influencing or causing such person, partnership or corporation to influence any elector of the state to vote for or against any candidate for public office or for nomination for public office or to any public officer for the purpose of influencing his official action, but nothing in this act shall be construed to restrain or abridge the liberty of the press or prohibit the consideration and discussion therein of candidacies, nominations, public officers or political questions. [32 G. A., ch. 73, § 1.]

Sec. 1641-i. **Solicitation from corporations** prohibited. It shall be unlawful for any member of any political committee, political party, or employe or representative thereof, or candidate for any office or the representative of such candidate, to solicit, request or knowingly receive from any corporation or any officer, agent or representative thereof, any money, property or thing of value belonging to such corporation, for campaign expenses or for any political purpose whatsoever. [32 G. A., ch. 73, § 2.]

Sec. 1641-j. **Testimony—immunity from prosecution.** No person, and no agent or officer of any corporation within the purview of this act shall be privileged from testifying in relation to anything herein prohibited; and no person having so testified shall be liable to any prosecution or punishment for any offense concerning which he is required to give his testimony, provided that he shall not be exempted from prosecution and punishment for perjury committed in so testifying. [32 G. A., ch. 73, § 3.]

Sec. 1641-k. **Penalty.** Any person convicted of a violation of any of the provisions of this act shall be punished by imprisonment in the county jail not less than six months or more than one year and in the discretion of the court, by fine not exceeding ten hundred dollars. [32 G. A., ch. 73, § 4.]

DIVISION XXV.

BRIBERY AND CORRUPTION IN ELECTIONS.

Section 4914. **Bribery of electors.** Any person offering or giving a bribe to any elector for the purpose of influencing his vote at any election authorized by law, or any elector entitled to vote at such election receiving such bribe, shall be fined not exceeding five hundred dollars, or imprisoned in the county jail not exceeding one year, or both.   [C. '73, § 3993; R., § 4333.]

Sec. 4915.   **To refrain from voting—to work for candidate.** If any person shall make an agreement with another to pay him any sum of money or other valuable thing in consideration that such other person shall refrain from voting at any election, or shall induce other qualified electors to refrain from voting, or that such other person shall perform any service or labor on any election day in the interest of any candidate for any office who is to be voted for at such election, or in the interest of any measure or political party, he shall be fined in any sum not less than fifty nor more than three hundred dollars, or be imprisoned in the county jail not exceeding ninety days. [25 G. A., ch. 59, § 1.]

Sec. 4916.   Accepting **bribe—punishment.** Any person who shall, in consideration of any sum of money or other valuable thing, agree to refrain from voting at any general or municipal election, or to induce or attempt to induce others to do so, or agree to perform on election day any service in the interest of any candidate, party or measure in consideration of any money or other valuable thing, or who shall accept any money or other valuable thing for such services performed in the interest of any candidate, political party or measure, shall be punished as provided in the preceding section.   [25 G. A., ch. 59, § 2.]

Sec. 4917.   **Contracts to convey voters.** Nothing in the two preceding sections shall be so construed as to punish individuals or committees of any political party from making contracts in good faith for the conveyance of voters to and from polling places and the payment of any reasonable compensation for such service.   [25 G. A., ch. 59, § 3.]

Sec. 1087-a32.   **Services for hire—penalty.** Any person who shall agree to perform any services in the interest of any candidate in consideration of any money or other valuable thing, or who shall accept any money or other valuable thing for such services performed in the interest of any candidate, or any person paying or offering to pay or giving or offering to give money or other valuable things for such services, shall be punished by a fine of not more than three hundred dollars, or by imprisonment in the county jail not exceeding ninety days. But nothing herein shall be construed to prohibit any person from making contracts in good faith for the announcement of his candidacy in the newspapers and for securing the names of voters required to file preliminary nomination papers and the payment of any reasonable compensation for such services. [32 G. A., ch. 51, § 32.]

Sec. 1087-a33.   Bribery—illegal voting—penalty.   Any person offering or giving a bribe, either in money or other consideration, to any elector for the purpose of influencing his vote at a primary election, or any elector entitled to vote at such primary election receiving and accepting such bribe; any person making false answer to any of the provisions of this act[1] relative to his qualifications and party affiliations; any person wilfully voting or offering to vote at a primary election who has not been a resident of this state for six months next preceding said primary election; or who, at the primary election, is not twenty-one years of age, or is not a citizen of the United States; or knowing himself not to be a qualified elector of such precinct where he offers to vote; or any person violating any of the provisions of this act,[2] or of any provisions of the code as may be hereto applied, and any person knowingly procuring, aiding or abetting such violation, shall be deemed guilty of a misdemeanor, and, upon conviction, shall be fined not less than one hundred dollars nor more than five hundred dollars, or be imprisoned in the county jail not less than thirty days nor more than six months.   [32 G. A., ch. 51, § 33.]

Sec. 4918.   Voting more than once.   If any elector unlawfully vote more than once at any election which may be held by virtue of any law of this state, he shall be fined not exceeding two hundred dollars, or be imprisoned in the county jail not exceeding one year.   [C. '73, § 3994; R., § 4334; C. '51, § 2692.]

Sec. 4919.   When not qualified. If any person, knowing himself not to be qualified, vote at any election authorized by law, he shall be fined not exceeding two hundred dollars, or be imprisoned in the county jail not exceeding six months.   [C. '73, § 3995; R., § 4335; C. '51, § 2693.]

Sec. 4920.   Residence in county.   If any person go or come into any county of this state, and vote in such county, not being a resident thereof, he shall be fined not exceeding two hundred

---

[1] See secs. 1087-a7, 1087-a8 and 1087-a9.
[2] Secs. 1087-a1 to 1087-a35, inclusive.

dollars, or be imprisoned in the county jail not exceeding one year. [C. '73, § 3996; R., § 4336; C. '51, § 2694.]

Sec. 4921. **Residence in state.** If any person wilfully vote who has not been a resident of this state for six months next preceding the election, or who, at the time of the election, is not twenty-one years of age, or who is not a citizen of the United States, or who is not qualified, by reason of other disability, to vote at the place where and time when the vote is to be given, he shall be fined in a sum not exceeding three hundred dollars, or imprisoned in the county jail not exceeding one year. [C. '73, § 3997; R., § 4337; C. '51, § 2695.]

Sec. 4922. **Counseling to vote when not qualified.** If any person procure, aid, assist, counsel or advise another to give his vote, knowing that such person is disqualified, he shall be fined not exceeding five hundred nor less than fifty dollars, and be imprisoned in the county jail not exceeding one year. [C. '73, § 3998; R., § 4338; C. '51, § 2696.]

Sec. 4923. **Deceiving voter as to ballot.** If any judge or clerk of election furnish an elector with a ticket or ballot, informing him that it contains a name or names different from those which are written or printed therein, with an intent to induce him to vote contrary to his inclination, or fraudulently or deceitfully change a ballot of any elector, by which such elector is deprived of voting for such candidate or person as he intended, he shall be imprisoned in the county jail not exceeding two years, and be fined not exceeding one thousand dollars nor less than one hundred dollars. [C. '73, § 3999; R., § 4339; C. '51, § 2697.]

Sec. 4924. **Preventing from voting by force or threats.** If any person unlawfully and by force, or threats of force, prevent, or endeavor to prevent, an elector from giving his vote at any public election, he shall be imprisoned in the county jail not exceeding six months, and fined not more than two hundred dollars. [C. '73, § 4000; R., § 4340; C. '51, § 2698.]

Sec. 4925. **Bribing clerks, judges, etc.** If any person give or offer a bribe to any judge, clerk or canvasser of any election authorized by law, or any executive officer attending the same, as a consideration for some act done or omitted to be done contrary to his official duty in relation to such election, he shall be fined not exceeding seven hundred dollars, and imprisoned in the county jail not exceeding one year. [C. '73, § 4001; R., § 4341; C. '51, § 2699.]

Sec. 4926. **Procuring vote by influence or threats.** If any person procure, or endeavor to procure, the vote of any elector, or the influence of any person over other electors, at any election, for himself, or for or against any candidate, by means of violence, threats of violence, or threats of withdrawing custom or dealing in business or trade, or enforcing the payment of debts, or bringing any civil or criminal action, or any other threat of injury to be inflicted by him or by his means, he shall be fined not exceeding five hundred dollars, or imprisoned in the county jail not more than one year. [C. '73, § 4002; R., § 4342; C. '51, § 2700.]

Sec. 4927. **Judges or clerks making false entries, etc.** If any judge or clerk of any election authorized by law knowingly make or consent to any false entry on the list of voters or poll books; or put into the ballot box, or permit to be so put in, any ballot not given by a voter; or take out of such box, or permit to be so taken out, any ballot deposited therein, except in the manner prescribed by law; or by any other act or omission designedly destroy or change the ballots given by the electors, he shall be fined not exceeding one thousand dollars, and imprisoned in the penitentiary not exceeding five years. [C. '73, § 4003; R., § 4343; C. '51, § 2701.]

Sec. 4928. **Illegally receiving or rejecting votes.** When any one who offers to vote at any election is objected to by an elector as a person not possessing the requisite qualifications, if any judge of such election unlawfully permit him to vote without producing proof of such qualification in the manner directed by law, or if any such judge wilfully refuse the vote of any person who complies with the requisites prescribed by law to prove his qualifications, he shall be fined not more than two hundred nor less than twenty dollars, or be imprisoned in the county jail not exceeding six months. [C. '73, § 4004; R., § 4344; C. '51, § 2702.]

Sec. 4929. **Misconduct to avoid election.** If any judge, clerk or executive officer designedly omit to do any official act required by law, or designedly do any illegal act, in relation to any public election, by which act or omission the votes taken at any such election in any city, town, precinct, township or district be lost, or the electors thereof be deprived of their

9

suffrage at such election, or designedly do any act which renders such election void, he shall be fined not less than one hundred nor more than one thousand dollars, or imprisoned in the county jail not more than one year, or both.   [C. '73, § 4005; R., § 4345; C. '51, § 2703.]

Sec. 4930.   **Not returning poll books.**   If any judge, clerk or messenger, after having been deputed by the judges of the election to carry the poll books of such election to the place where by law they are to be canvassed, wilfully or negligently fail to deliver them within the time prescribed by law, safe, with the seal unbroken, he shall, for every such offense, be fined not more than five hundred nor less than fifty dollars. [C. '73, § 4006; R., § 4346; C. '51, § 2704.]

Sec. 4931.   **Improper registry.**   Any person who causes his name to be registered, knowing that he is not or will not become a qualified voter in the precinct where his name is registered previous to the next election, or who shall wrongfully personate any registered voter, and any person causing, or aiding or abetting any person in either of said acts, shall be, for each offense, imprisoned in the penitentiary not less than one year.   [C. '73, § 4007.]

Sec. 1136.   **Forgery of papers or ballots.**   Any person who shall falsely make, or wilfully destroy, any certificate of nomination or nomination papers, or any part thereof, or any letter of withdrawal, or file any certificate of nomination, or nomination papers, knowing the same or any part thereof to be falsely made, or suppress any certificate of nomination, or nomination papers, or any part thereof, which have been duly filed, or forge or falsely make the official indorsement on any ballot, or substitute therefor any spurious or counterfeit ballot, or make, use, circulate, or cause to be made or circulated as an official ballot, any paper printed in imitation or resemblance thereof, or wilfully destroy or deface any ballot, or wilfully delay the delivery of any ballots, shall be punished by a fine of not less than one hundred nor more than one thousand dollars, or by imprisonment in the penitentiary not less than one nor more than five years, or by both fine and imprisonment. [24 G. A., ch. 33, § 29.]

Sec. 4931-a.   **Political advertisements, etc., to be signed— penalty.**   Whoever writes, prints, posts or distributes, or causes to be written, printed, posted or distributed, a circular, poster or advertisement which is designed to promote the nomination or election of a candidate for public office or to injure and defeat the nomination or election of any candidate for public office, or to influence the voters on any constitutional amendment, or to influence the vote of any member of the legislature, unless there appears upon such circular or poster or advertisement, in a conspicuous place, either the name of the chairman or secretary or of two officers of the organization issuing the same, or of the person who is responsible therefor, with his name and address, shall be guilty of a misdemeanor and upon conviction thereof shall be fined not exceeding one hundred dollars, or imprisoned in the county jail not to exceed thirty days, or by both such fine and imprisonment.

Provided, that nothing in this act shall apply to the editorial or news advertisements of any magazine or newspaper where the same is not a political advertisement, nor to cards, posters, lithographs or circulars, issued by a candidate advertising his own candidacy. [36 G. A., ch. 243, § 1.]

Sec. 4919-a. Illegal voting. Whenever any political party shall hold a primary election for the purpose of nominating a candidate for any public office or for the purpose of selecting delegates to any convention of such party, it shall be unlawful for any person not a qualified elector, or any qualified elector not at the time a member in good faith of such political party, to vote at such primary election. Any person violating the provisions of this section, and any person knowingly procuring, aiding or abetting such violation, shall be deemed guilty of a misdemeanor, and upon conviction shall be fined not to exceed one hundred dollars or be imprisoned in the county jail not to exceed thirty days. [27 G. A., ch. 111, § 1.]

Sec. 4919-b. Prima facie evidence. It shall be prima facie evidence of the violation of the preceding section for any person who has participated in any primary election of one political party, to vote at a primary election held by another political party, to select candidates to be voted for at the same election; or to select delegates to any convention of the party holding such primary election. [27 G. A., ch. 111, § 2.]

Sec. 4919-c. Authority to administer oaths. Any judge of such primary election shall have power to administer oaths to, and to examine under oath, any person offering to vote at such election, touching his qualifications to participate in such primary election, and it shall be the duty of such judge of election to so examine or cause to be examined any person challenged as to his right to vote. Any person testifying falsely as to any material matter, touching his qualifications to participate in such primary election, shall be deemed guilty of perjury and punished accordingly. [27 G. A., ch. 111, § 3.]

Sec. **4919-d.** What **excepted.** Nothing in this act shall be construed to apply to conventions held under the caucus system. [27 G. A., ch. 111, § 4.]

INDEX

11

Voting:

Voting Booths: